ZOMBIE CINEMA

QUICK TAKES: MOVIES AND POPULAR CULTURE

Quick Takes: Movies and Popular Culture is a series offering succinct overviews and high-quality writing on cutting-edge themes and issues in film studies. Authors offer both fresh perspectives on new areas of inquiry and original takes on established topics.

SERIES EDITORS:

Gwendolyn Audrey Foster is Willa Cather Professor of English, and she teaches film studies in the Department of English at the University of Nebraska, Lincoln.

Wheeler Winston Dixon is the James Ryan Endowed Professor of Film Studies and Professor of English at the University of Nebraska, Lincoln.

Ian Olney, *Zombie Cinema*
Valérie K. Orlando, *New African Cinema*
Steven Shaviro, *Digital Music Videos*
John Wills, *Disney Culture*

Zombie Cinema

IAN OLNEY

RUTGERS UNIVERSITY PRESS
New Brunswick, Camden, and Newark, New Jersey, and London

Library of Congress Cataloging-in-Publication Data
Names: Olney, Ian.
Title: Zombie cinema / Ian Olney.
Description: New Brunswick : Rutgers University Press,
2017. | Series: Quick takes: movies and popular culture |
Includes bibliographical references and index.
Identifiers: LCCN 2016033640| ISBN 9780813579474
(pbk. : alk. paper) | ISBN 9780813579481 (e-book) |
ISBN 9780813579498 (e-book (web pdf))
Subjects: LCSH: Zombie films—History and criticism. |
Zombies in motion pictures.
Classification: LCC PN1995.9.Z63 O46 2017 |
DDC 791.43/675—dc23
LC record available at https://lccn.loc.gov/2016033640

A British Cataloging-in-Publication record for this book is
available from the British Library.

∞ The paper used in this publication meets the requirements of the
American National Standard for Information Sciences—
Permanence of Paper for Printed Library Materials,
ANSI Z39.48–1992.

www.rutgersuniversitypress.org

Manufactured in the United States of America

CONTENTS

ZOMBIE CINEMA

INTRODUCTION
Our Zombies, Ourselves

It's official: the zombie apocalypse is here. The living dead have been lurking in media and popular culture since the 1930s, but they have never been as ubiquitous or as widely embraced as they are today. This is especially true in cinema. Movie screens teem with zombies of all kinds: fast zombies and slow zombies, flesh-eating zombies and brain-eating zombies, plague zombies and rage zombies, voodoo zombies and demonic zombies, teen zombies and period zombies, redneck zombies and Nazi zombies, sex zombies and pet zombies. They appear in everything from Hollywood blockbusters like *I Am Legend* (2007) and *World War Z* (2013) to offbeat indie movies like *Pontypool* (2008) and *It Follows* (2014) to straight-to-video schlock like *Flight of the Living Dead* (2007) and *Abraham Lincoln vs. Zombies* (2012). They have overrun almost every genre imaginable, including science fiction (*The Last Days on Mars*, 2013), teen comedy (*Scouts Guide to the Zombie Apocalypse*, 2015), the western (*Jonah Hex*,

2010), family melodrama (*Maggie*, 2015), romantic comedy (*Warm Bodies*, 2013), literary adaptation (*Pride and Prejudice and Zombies*, 2016), animation (*ParaNorman*, 2012)—even pornography, gay (*Otto; or, Up with Dead People*, 2008) and straight (*Dawna of the Dead*, 2010). And they have gone global, spreading well beyond the borders of North American and western European cinema to turn up in films from countries as far-flung as Japan, Norway, New Zealand, India, Turkey, Cuba, and Nigeria. The sheer number of zombie movies made just in the past decade or so is astonishing: more films featuring the living dead have been released around the world since 2005 than in the previous seven decades combined (Russell 186).

The zombie apocalypse has by no means been confined to the big screen, however. Recent years have seen an explosion in television shows about the living dead as well. Most prominent among them is AMC's *The Walking Dead* (2010–), based on a series of graphic novels created by Robert Kirkman. The show, which focuses on a southern small-town sheriff's deputy who leads a band of survivors in the wake of a zombie outbreak, has become the most watched program in the history of cable TV, its season 5 premiere drawing a record 17.2 million live viewers in October of 2014 (St. John). *Fear the Walking Dead* (2015–), a spin-off following the fortunes of a family from Los Angeles during the early days of the outbreak, also commands a huge audience; its first episode, which aired in August 2015, was the highest-rated cable series launch ever, with 10.1 million viewers (Kissell). While the *Walking Dead* franchise is undoubtedly the most popular example of zombie programming on television, it is far from the only one. It was preceded by *Dead Set* (2008), a British miniseries in which zombies interrupt taping on the reality TV show *Big Brother* (2000–). And it has been joined by many other programs since its debut, from *The Returned* (*Les revenants*, 2012–), a somber French drama about a rural mountain community whose dead mysteriously begin to return from the grave and resume their old lives, to *iZombie* (2015–), a comedy on The CW about a zombified med student who takes a job at the morgue, where she satisfies her craving for fresh brains and helps solve murder cases. Television, like cinema, has become an industry of the living dead.

Nor does the apocalypse end there. Film and TV (including home video and video on demand) are just the tip of a zombie economy worth an estimated $5.74 billion a year (Ogg). The dead have spread to video games, swarming across a range of genres (first-person shooter games, open world survival games, tower defense games, massively multiplayer online games) and platforms (consoles, PCs, tablets, smartphones) in titles like *Left 4 Dead*, *Call of Duty: World at War*, *Dead Rising*, and *Plants vs. Zombies.* Many zombie video games have spawned franchises as durable as any in cinema; a few—*Resident Evil, House of the Dead, Doom*—have actually been made into movies, demonstrating that the zombie economy is (fittingly) cannibalistic, feeding on itself to fuel its own growth. The dead also infest popular fiction, shambling through such best-sellers as Max Brooks's *World War Z: An Oral History of the Zombie War*, Seth Grahame-Smith's *Pride and Prejudice and Zombies*, Colson Whitehead's *Zone One*, and Stephen King's *Cell: A Novel.* They have invaded graphic novels like Kirkman's *The Walking Dead* and Chris Roberson and Michael Allred's *iZOMBIE* and even infiltrated time-honored comics like the *Marvel Super-Heroes* and *Archie* series, both of which have recently undergone zombie makeovers. Once again, a number of these books have returned as films and television shows, proving as undead as their subjects. But the larger zombie marketplace encompasses more than books and video games. There are apps for our mobile devices that allow us to practice our zombie headshots (Dead Trigger), stay fit by fleeing virtual zombie hordes (Zombies, Run!), and zombify photos of ourselves and our friends (ZombieBooth: 3D Zombifier). There are zombie-themed restaurants, amusement parks, cruises, and boot camps to occupy our leisure time. There is zombie art, zombie music, and zombie theater for our entertainment. And there is an endless assortment of zombie novelty items for us to buy, including costumes, toys, T-shirts, posters, coffee mugs, bumper stickers, key chains—the list goes on and on. The living dead are a big business.

Yet the twenty-first-century zombie apocalypse also extends beyond the economy. The dead haven't simply cornered the market; they have conquered contemporary culture, colonizing the popular imagination. This is perhaps most evident in the burgeoning growth of zombie fandom worldwide. Devotees of the living dead flock annually to international conventions like ZomBcon and Walker Stalker Con, where they mingle with fellow zombie lovers, browse booths run by zombie vendors, attend zombie panels and Q&As, meet zombie celebrities, and engage in zombie cosplay, dressing up as their favorite monster. In drag as the dead, they gather in the thousands to stage massive Zombie Walks in cities around the globe, including Toronto, Pittsburgh, Buenos Aires, Seattle, Brisbane, Dublin, Minneapolis, and Santiago. They also congregate online, using websites, blogs, and discussion groups, as well as social media networks like Facebook, Twitter, YouTube, and Instagram, to proclaim their passion for the living dead and to share their zombie fan art, fan fiction, and fan films. Zombie culture doesn't stop at hardcore fandom, though; it has seeped into the quotidian. Communities sponsor Zombie Walks and 5K Runs for charity. Weekend warriors form clubs to drill for the zombie apocalypse in their free time. Universities and colleges offer courses on the living dead. Public health institutes use the zombie outbreak to illustrate the importance of emergency preparedness. Most strikingly, zombieism has become a dominant cultural metaphor—a lens through which we view the world in virtually every walk of life. In finance we speak of zombie banks, in real estate we speak of zombie homes, in politics we speak of zombie candidates, in philosophy we speak of zombie consciousness, and in biology we speak of zombie wasps. We have woven the dead deeply into the fabric of our daily existence.

The question is, Why? Why do the dead so dominate life in the twenty-first century? They were not always this central to our existence. True, zombies have had a long run in media and popular culture. First emerging as slaves of voodoo in B horror movies like *White Zombie* (1932) and *I Walked with a Zombie* (1943), they persisted in cinema throughout the last century in one form or another. When the Cold War broke out, they were reimagined as robotic victims of alien mind control in such science-fiction films as *Invasion of the Body Snatchers* (1956) and *The Earth Dies Screaming* (1964). During the darkest days of the Vietnam War era, George A. Romero's seminal *Night of the Living Dead* (1968) transformed them into flesh-eating ghouls. At the dawn of the video age, they became staples of splatter horror in gore movies like *The Evil Dead* (1981) and *The Beyond* (. . . *E tu vivrai nel terrore! L'aldilà,* 1981). And as the century drew to a close, they were repurposed as avatars of postmodern angst in such low-budget, indie films as *Shatter Dead* (1993) and *I, Zombie: The Chronicles of Pain* (1998). Zombies also made a splash as undead avengers in the 1950s EC Comics series *Tales from the Crypt,* as undead dancers in the 1980s Michael Jackson music video *Thriller,* and as undead biohazards in the 1990s Capcom video game *Resident Evil.* Despite the persistence of zombies in media and popular culture over course of the twentieth century, however, they never really captured the public's imagination the way that, say, vampires or serial killers did. As Jamie Russell notes, zombies were generally regarded as the "great unwashed of horror cinema" (6) and by the end of the century had fallen distinctly out of favor with audiences (120). Their phenomenal popularity in the new millennium, then, represents a remarkable reversal of fortune. What explains it?

Judging from the substantial body of commentary that the zombie's twenty-first-century renaissance has generated, the leading theory seems to be that the dead resonate with audiences today because they embody contemporary fears and desires. On one hand, they act as a "barometer of cultural anxiety" (Dendle), reflecting current worries about terrorism and social collapse (Muntean and Payne), economic recession and downward social mobility (Bosch), globalization and illicit border crossings (Saunders), and infectious disease and global pandemics (Klein). On the other, they permit a kind of cultural wish fulfillment, catering to current fantasies about life in a postapocalyptic world without social structures or laws, where survival is paramount and violence is not simply permitted but necessary and justified (Bishop, "Dead" 21–22). In short, the zombie functions, to quote Kyle Bishop, as "the ultimate foreign Other" ("Raising" 201)—a figure whose utter difference from us enables it to act as vehicle for our worries and our wants. This, the argument goes, is the root of zombie culture's modern appeal. It provides a safe space for us to face the things we fear or desire in the new millennium, allowing us to grapple with them in a purely symbolic fashion. The dead have operated in this way before. For example, in the landmark essay "An Introduction to the American Horror Film," which pioneered the notion of the horror-movie monster as Other, Robin Wood establishes that in the late sixties the zombie spoke to America's concerns about its countercultural youth, who seemed poised to devour the older generation (17). But critics contend that the zombie's key attributes—its uncanny reanimation, mindless mobbing, gruesome cannibalism, and terrifying contagiousness—chime especially well with our anxieties and fantasies today, making it an ideal Other for the twenty-first century.

There is no doubt some truth to this view. As an explanation for the zombie's renaissance in the new millennium, however, it seems to me incomplete. For when I survey contemporary zombie culture, I am struck by how much of it is driven by an *identification with* the living dead. Over the past decade or so, there has been a pronounced shift in our public conception of the zombie: increasingly, it has come to serve not as a symbolic Other but as a symbolic Self. Stephen Shapiro describes this development as an "accelerating turn in zombie works toward a Janus-like form of representation, where the viewer's emotional alignment, her affective point of view, has become increasingly both *against* and *with* the zombie in ways suggesting that the impulse to be 'versus' the zombie and splatter its stuffing is now joined with a longing to *be* the zombie, to walk *in*, rather than alongside, its shoes" (217).

Such a yearning is evident in the cosplay at zombie conventions and Zombie Walks. It's evident in the popularity of mobile apps that allow us to zombify photos of ourselves and our friends. It's evident in the rise of restaurants offering zombie-themed dishes like fake brains. Maybe most tellingly, it's evident in the growing number of movies and TV shows that feature zombie heroes—from the aforementioned *Jonah Hex, Maggie, Warm Bodies, Otto; or, Up with Dead People, Dawna of the Dead, The Returned,* and *iZombie* to *Fido* (2006), *Zombies Anonymous* (2006), *American Zombie* (2007), *Aaah! Zombies!!* (2007), *Colin* (2008), *The Revenant* (2009), *DeadHeads* (2011), *Harold's Going Stiff* (2011), *A Little Bit Zombie* (2012), *Contracted* (2013), *Pretty Dead* (2013), *Freaks of Nature* (2015), *In the Flesh* (2013–2014), and *Z Nation* (2014–). All this points to a fascinating possibility: that the mass appeal of the living dead today is rooted not in our perception of their difference from us, chiefly, but in our recognition that on a fundamental level they *are* us.

One might argue that this does not make them unique. Over the years, audiences have identified with other horror-movie monsters; some have become cultural icons as a result. Even now, hit films and television series elicit our empathy for vampires (the *Twilight* franchise, 2008–2012), werewolves (*Teen Wolf,* 2011–), Frankenstein monsters (*I, Frankenstein,* 2014), and serial killers (*Hannibal,* 2013–2015). But the current zombie apocalypse tells us that the living dead are different. The level of popularity they have attained in the twenty-first century is unprecedented—not just for zombies but for any monster. They are more than iconic; they are emblematic.

Our wholesale embrace of zombies in the new millennium suggests that we see something of ourselves in them that we don't see in other monsters. It also suggests that they capture who we are not simply as individuals but as a society.

That, in a nutshell, is the case I make in this book. Without denying that the dead have frequently represented "them" in media and popular culture, I focus on how they can be said to embody "us." Literally, of course, zombies are us—or at least they once were. That is, they used to be human. And we have always had a closer kinship with the living dead than with other horror-movie monsters. In contrast to the aristocratic vampire or the brilliant serial killer, zombies are like most of us: ordinary and unremarkable. As George A. Romero is fond of putting it, zombies are "blue-collar monster[s]" (Keough 174)—they are "the neighbors" (Yakir 62). But I argue that we share an even more elemental connection with the dead, especially those of us living in the West, where the modern zombie was born and today reigns supreme. Simply put, the dead illustrate who we are as a society. Zombie culture functions like a funhouse mirror, reflecting our dominant social order—white, capitalist, and patriarchal—as a kind of living death: insatiably rapacious and perversely enduring. This is nothing new. The dead have reflected life in the West since they first emerged in media and popular culture over eighty years ago. What has changed is our willingness to look into the mirror.

Among other things, the twenty-first-century zombie apocalypse signifies a new acknowledgment on the part of cultural consumers and producers that, as a song from the Australian death metal band Black Jesus has it, "we're all zombies now." Prompted, perhaps, by the growing number of challenges to the dominant social order in the new millennium—many in the form of grassroots movements like Occupy Wall Street, Black Lives Matter, and One Billion Rising—we have embraced zombie culture as a space to contemplate our "postmortem condition." This is not an idea that has received the kind of sustained attention it deserves in scholarly writing on the living dead, the titles of several recent books (*Generation Zombie, Thinking Dead, Zombies Are Us*) notwithstanding. By and large, critics continue to see zombies as irreducibly Other. My goal is to show that if Gilles Deleuze and Félix Guattari are correct in their famous assertion that "the only modern myth is the myth of zombies" (335), it's in part because zombie culture reveals that our zombies are ourselves.

This is particularly true of zombie cinema, which not only launched the living dead in media and popular culture but has also proven to be their most enduring and important platform. Over time, zombie movies—and television shows—have closely tracked the evolution of our modern zombiehood, capturing the ways in which the dominant social order in the West exemplifies a kind of living death. In the chapters that follow, I explore how they have done so. I begin in chapter 1 with a consideration of whiteness and living death, arguing that zombie cinema, as its roots in colonialism attest, has much to tell us about the role that race and racism have played in the zombification of Western culture. Chapter 2 focuses on living death and capitalism, suggesting that in the zombie film's representation of the zombie as consumer and consumed, a monster driven and destroyed by its appetite, we find an apt metaphor for another key aspect of our postmortem condition. Chapter 3 looks at patriarchy and living death, locating in zombie cinema's treatment of gender and sexuality a commentary on the connection between regressive masculinity and our modern zombiehood. I end with a conclusion examining living death and dispossession, contending that zombie television has taken the loss of home as its central conceit in order to register the point of crisis at which the dominant social order in the West now finds itself.

As a "quick take" on zombie cinema, this short book can't hope to be comprehensive or exhaustive in its coverage of the living dead in film and on television. Nor does it aim to be. It is purposely focused in its critical approach, which might best be described as sociopolitical, attuned as it is to the ideological implications of zombie cinema. This is not the only methodology that can help us make sense of filmic and televisual representations of the living dead, to be sure; other approaches, from the psychological to the philosophical, have illuminated key facets of zombie cinema. But it is, I think, the one that best accounts for the astonishing popularity of the dead in contemporary Western culture. This book is also deliberately selective in its discussion of zombie film and TV. Although it makes room for the offbeat, the contested, and the forgotten, it focuses on the canonical texts of zombie cinema. Likewise, while it does not ignore the newly global reach of the living dead, its emphasis is on zombie movies and TV shows from North America and western Europe. This is partly because space for discussion is limited and readers are most likely to be familiar with the "greatest hits" of zombie cinema. More importantly, however, it is because these works offer the clearest reflection of the living death that the West has fashioned for itself. It is from them, ultimately, that we learn why our hunger for zombies, like their hunger for us, seems insatiable in the twenty-first century.

1

BLACK MASK, WHITE ZOMBIES

Unlike most classic movie monsters, whose origins lie in European Gothic literature, the zombie has its roots in Afro-Caribbean folklore. It is, as Sarah Juliet Lauro observes, a uniquely "transatlantic" figure (*Transatlantic*). The word "zombie" or "zombi" (as it was originally spelled) can be traced back to West Africa. Although its etymology is uncertain—it may derive from *nzambi* or *zumbi*, Congolese terms used for the spirit of a dead person and a fetish charm, respectively—Hans-W. Ackermann and Jeanine Gauthier demonstrate that it initially had a dual meaning, referring not only to a body without a soul but also to a soul without a body (473); indeed, it seems to have been primarily connected with the notion of a spirit influenced or captured through magic (490). It became definitively attached to the concept of living death only with its migration to the New World, which occurred as a result of the Atlantic slave trade.

Of the millions of West Africans forced into bondage in the seventeenth and eighteenth centuries, many were shipped to European colonies in the Caribbean, where their ancestral beliefs gradually blended with those of the Christian colonizers, forming syncretic religions. It was one such faith, Vaudou, observed in secret by slaves laboring in the French colony on Saint-Domingue, that recast the zombie as a dead body reanimated by a sorcerer and pressed into perpetual servitude. Zombification was a source of horror for practitioners of Vaudou, for whom it represented an extension in death of the bondage they suffered in life. Even after a successful slave rebellion established Saint-Domingue as a free "Black Republic"— renamed Haiti—in 1804, it remained a vital part of Vaudoun folklore and a very real fear, famously enshrined as a criminal act under Article 246 of the country's penal code in 1864.

The zombie remained virtually unknown outside Haiti, however. It was not introduced to the rest of the world until the 1920s, a decade when interest in Haiti ran high—especially in the United States, which had invaded and occupied the country in 1915. Allegedly undertaken to protect American interests from the political instability plaguing the island, these actions were actually part of an expansionist foreign policy plan that, as Gary D. Rhodes notes, "allowed the U.S. to become the premier power in the Caribbean under the guise of installing a liberal democracy for the first time in Haiti" (71). Lasting almost twenty years, the occupation prompted countless newspaper stories, magazine articles, and books about Haiti in America; most painted the nation "as an impoverished land of throbbing drums, ruled by pretentious buffoons and populated by swamp doctors, licentious women, and children bred for the cauldron," reassuring the public that "any country where such abominations took place could find its salvation only through military occupation" (Davis 73).

Among these pieces was William Seabrook's 1929 travelogue *The Magic Island*, which titillated readers with tales of dead men working in Haitian cane fields, becoming the first English-language publication to describe reanimated bodies as "zombies." The book was a sensation, cementing the zombie as an emblem of "voodoo"—as Vaudou was called in the United States—and launching the monster as a pop-culture icon. It inspired everything from a Broadway play (scripted by Kenneth Webb) to a notoriously potent cocktail (concocted by Donn Beach). Its biggest impact, though, was in cinema, where it spawned a new type of horror movie: the zombie film.

Most early zombie films emphatically foreground the zombie's Afro-Caribbean origins. Typically set in the colonial West Indies, they revolve around the use of black magic to raise the dead and control the living, explicitly framing the zombie as a raced horror monster. Not surprisingly, critics tend to see these films as an extension of the racist and imperialist discourse surrounding the American occupation of Haiti—and, more broadly, as a legacy of the centuries-old project of Western colonialism. After all, these movies owe their existence to a book that provided cover for America's imperial ambitions in Haiti by presenting Vaudoun beliefs as evidence of the Black Republic's backwardness and savagery. And *The Magic Island* was just the latest in a long line of American and European texts stretching back to the beginning of the nineteenth century that, in the wake of Haiti's revolution, "promoted rumors of occult practices like grave-robbing and Vaudou potions that could make people appear dead temporarily" in order to "denigrate the Haitian as backward and (in an obvious lament of the loss of colonial domination over the region) incapable of self-rule" (Lauro, *Transatlantic* 48). As depicted by Seabrook, the zombie "did the same kind of ideological work as the cannibal—it was a new means of separating the world into its civilized and barbaric categories," of "cast[ing] Haitians, and by extension any peoples of color, as less than human" (Kee 22–23). It is no wonder, then, that the zombie films it inspired have often been read as carrying that work forward, as further refashioning a figure from Afro-Caribbean folklore into a symbol of racial Otherness; they seem to represent a clear example of the "persistence of colonialism in cultural form" (Lauro, *Transatlantic* 11).

Without disputing the fact that zombie cinema was fundamentally shaped by colonialism—or that it has at times served colonialist interests—I make a different argument in the pages that follow. This chapter explores the ways in which zombie movies, not just early on but right up to the present, have linked living death to whiteness, framing the figure of the zombie not as the black Other but as the white Self. Riffing on Frantz Fanon's *Black Skin, White Masks*, a landmark study of the psychology of the colonized subject, who is faced with a double bind—the necessity of disavowing one's racial identity and adopting that of the colonizer (donning a white mask) and the impossibility of ever escaping the visual marker of one's race (shedding black skin)—I argue that while zombie cinema may frequently wear a "black mask," appearing to concern itself chiefly with the theme of black Otherness, it actually establishes (literally or metaphorically, deliberately or not) that the real zombies are white. Observing that horror is by and large a "white genre in the West," dealing with the notion of "whites as both themselves dead and as bringers of death," Richard Dyer has speculated that it provides a "cultural space that makes bearable for whites the exploration of the association of whiteness with death" (210). That is precisely the claim I want to make about the zombie film: that it invites contemplation of white deathliness, specifically in connection with the West's treatment of racial Others, from the colonial era to our own age of neocolonialism. While its representations of blackness have changed over time, zombie cinema has been remarkably consistent in portraying whites as dead and bringers of death. If the folkloric zombie, born out of "the experience of slavery, the sea passage from Africa to the New World, and revolution on the soil of Saint-Domingue, . . . tells the story of colonization" (Dayan 36–37), the cinematic zombie reveals that, as René Depestre writes, the "history of colonization is the process of man's general zombification" (qtd. in McAlister 108)—that the colonizer, too, is made monstrous by the experience of colonialism.

This theme announces itself in the title of the first zombie movie ever made, inaugurating zombie cinema's colonial phase: *White Zombie* (1932). An independent picture shot for a mere $60,000 in less than two weeks (Rhodes 91, 104) and distributed through United Artists, *White Zombie* was designed by its director and producer—brothers Victor and Edward Halperin—to capitalize on the popularity of *The Magic Island*, as well as the commercial success of two pioneering horror films released by Universal Studios: Tod Browning's *Dracula* (1931) and James Whale's *Frankenstein* (1931). Working with the screenwriter Garnett Weston, the Halperin brothers repurposed the Haitian zombie as a movie monster and placed it at the center of a Gothic story in the Universal mold. The plot revolves around a hypnotic villain—Murder Legendre, played by the *Dracula* star Bela Lugosi—who operates a sugar mill in Haiti using zombie workers he has enslaved; when he zombifies a young white woman, Madeline (Madge Bellamy), his reign of terror is brought to an end by her husband, Neil (John Harron), with the aid of a sagacious Christian missionary, Dr. Bruner (Joseph Cawthorn).

At first glance, *White Zombie* may seem to mirror *The Magic Island* in its presentation of Vaudoun folklore and the Haitian people. Certainly, scholars have viewed the film as trafficking in colonialist images of racial Otherness. Kyle Bishop writes that it "uses the exotic setting of Haiti to entrance eager viewers while accentuating the prevailing stereotypes of the 'backwards' natives and western imperialist superiority" ("Sub-Subaltern" 141). Likewise, Jamie Russell argues that the movie portrays Haitian culture as "only a few steps removed from outright savagery" (24), while Robin R. Means Coleman pronounces it, quite simply, an "indictment on Blackness" (53).

On closer inspection, however, it becomes clear that *White Zombie* is an indictment not of blackness but of whiteness. Indeed, it hardly deals with blackness at all. Bishop suggests that the film's zombies represent the "sub-subaltern" colonized subject, "literally silent, enslaved, and unable to connect with the dominant culture through any liminal space of discourse" ("Sub-Subaltern" 141). But with the exception of a handful of black zombies briefly shown among the ranks of the living dead working in the villain's sugar mill, all of the zombies in the movie are coded as white—that is, they are played by white actors wearing makeup designed to emphasize their ghoulishness (not blackface, as some critics have asserted). This includes the zombies we see most often in the movie: Legendre's six henchmen, some of whom he reveals were once part of the island's ruling class (the minister of the interior, the captain of the gendarmes, and the high executioner). Another is his former master, a witch doctor from whom he extracted the secrets of zombification. We might expect these zombies to be black, given Haitian history and culture, yet they are not. And then, of course, there is the film's eponymous zombie: Madeline, who, blond, pallid, and dressed in snowy robes, is the epitome of whiteness. True to the film's title, *White Zombie* offers us a picture of living death that is blindingly white.

So, too, is its picture of the "dark art" of voodoo. A number of commentators have claimed that Madeline's zombification is symptomatic of the movie's racism and imperialism, as it speaks to Western fears about the "unnatural displacement of white autonomy, supremacy, and control and the threat of sexual subjugation or miscegenation" embodied by the specter of the insubordinate black male native (Phillips 28). The exploitative advertising created for the film seems to support such a reading, with taglines like "A White Girl Caught in the Zombie Spell—Slave to the Evil Will of the Master Zombie!" A closer look, though, reveals that once again blackness is not at issue. While the zombie master portrayed by the European actor Bela Lugosi has been described as creole (or even, inexplicably, as black), his Western garb, elaborate Vandyke beard, and Hungarian-accented English clearly mark him as white. His powers of mesmerism, evoked by a gigantic close-up of his glowing eyes superimposed over the action on screen at various points in the movie, are not those of the colonized but those of the colonizer. In contrast to *The Magic Island*, *White Zombie* whitewashes black magic, linking voodoo practices, and the stigma attached to them, with Western imperialism.

It may be tempting to chalk this up to a disavowal of the true history of colonialism or to an erasure of blackness; both were endemic in Hollywood cinema at the time of the film's release. But there actually are black characters in *White Zombie*—beyond the briefly glimpsed zombies mentioned earlier—and I would submit that they too help to reinforce its representation of whites as dead and bringers of death. The movie is bookended by two key sequences featuring native Haitians. It opens with group of peasants conducting a funeral in the middle of a country road; as they finish filling in the graves, a coach bearing Madeline and Neil passes through. The black driver, played with quiet dignity by the African American actor Clarence Muse, explains to the couple that natives bury their loved ones in busy thoroughfares to protect them from "the men who steal dead bodies." Further down the road, they encounter the body snatchers themselves: Legendre and his zombie minions. After carrying Madeline and Neil safely past, the driver warns them that these white men are the living dead. The connection between whiteness and living death introduced in this early scene is cemented late in the film by a Haitian witch doctor (the only part in the movie obviously assayed by a white actor in blackface) who reveals to Dr. Bruner the location of Legendre's cliff-side castle, calling it "the land of the living dead." Despite the status of the driver and the witch doctor as minor characters, they play an important role in identifying where the real evil in Haiti lies: not with "savage" blacks but with "civilized" whites. One could even argue that their limited screen time (and the general dearth of black characters in the film) serves to suggest that the whole project of Western imperialism is founded on white fantasies of racial and cultural superiority rather than on any sort of empirical reality—that it has nothing to do with actual blackness at all.

White Zombie is by no means uniformly progressive in its treatment of race and colonialism; it is an ambiguous, even incoherent, text. At times, it trades in the kind of racism and imperialism one finds in other American movies of the period. Dr. Bruner, the film's voice of white, Western wisdom, pronounces Haiti "full of nonsense and superstition" and ascribes Madeline's zombification to "native work." And the requisite happy ending, which finds Legendre defeated and Madeline reunited with Neil, arguably works to reestablish whiteness as a racial norm and revalorize the project of Western imperialism. Yet, as we have seen, *White Zombie* also cuts against the grain of the era's dominant discourse on race and colonialism. Positioning whites as both zombie and zombie master, it reimagines the colonial scenario as one in which the colonizer is also the colonized, exposing colonialism as a zero-sum game that dehumanizes all parties involved. Regardless of whether its anticolonialist bent is a happy accident or the result of deliberate subversion, it opens a space for audiences to contemplate not only the deathliness of whiteness but also the self-defeating nature of Western imperialism.

White Zombie's indictment of whiteness set the template for many of the colonial zombie films that followed. Most prominent among them is Jacques Tourneur's *I Walked with a Zombie* (1943), produced by Val Lewton at RKO. Lewton's B horror unit was charged by the studio head, Charles Koerner, with turning out, as cheaply as possible, monster movies of the type popularized by Universal Studios. Each picture had to cost less than $150,000, run under seventy-five minutes, and carry an audience-tested title provided by the marketing department (Bansak 89). Despite these strictures, Lewton, a cultured and conscientious producer, managed to create a string of horror films in the 1940s that are infused with poetry and layered with meaning, making them in many ways the antithesis of Universal's more straightforward fare. This is especially true of his collaborations with Tourneur, which, as Chris Fujiwara writes, are at bottom about "the antagonisms and misunderstandings that arise from cultural difference," focusing on "normal, uncomplicated North Americans who become embroiled in doubt, guilt, and moral ambiguity through contact with a foreign culture" (6).

I Walked with a Zombie is a case in point. Although the title was foisted on Lewton and Tourneur, along with a story idea in the form of a sensationalistic article on voodoo practices penned by Inez Wallace for *American Weekly* magazine, they fashioned the movie into what Gwendolyn Audrey Foster aptly describes as a "devastating critique of whiteness and colonialism" ("Corruption" 149). It revolves in part around the moral education of its white heroine, a young Canadian nurse, Betsy Connell (Frances Dee), who is dispatched to the Caribbean island of Saint Sebastian to care for the invalid wife of a sugar planter named Paul Holland (Tom Conway). Initially blind to the island's ghastly legacy as an outpost of Western imperialism, Betsy gradually comes to see Saint Sebastian as the nightmarish place that J. Roy Hunt's shadowy black-and-white cinematography suggests it is.

Over the course of the film, Betsy's eyes are opened not only to the plight of its colonized but also to the monstrousness of its colonizers. She learns about its brutal history of slavery, symbolized by a statue of Saint Sebastian at Fort Holland that is known to black locals as Ti-Misery because it was once the figurehead of the slave ship that brought their ancestors to the island in chains. She also discovers the ugly truth that her patient, Paul's mute and mindless wife, Jessica (Christine Gordon), was zombified by his missionary mother, Mrs. Rand (Edith Barrett), when she threatened to leave Paul for his half brother, Wesley (James Ellison). As in *White Zombie*, white colonials emerge not as agents of civilization or enlightenment but as dead and bringers of death. Betsy's exposure to the deathliness of whiteness and the horrors of colonialism is one facet of her moral education in the movie.

Another facet is her contact with Saint Sebastian's black culture, which has a transformative impact on her perspective as a white outsider. The island's black inhabitants raise Betsy's awareness about its legacy of white violence and subjugation: the coachman (Clinton Rosemond) who drives her to Fort Holland upon her arrival informs her about the historical significance of Ti-Misery, for example, while a local calypso singer (Sir Lancelot) serenades her with a folk ballad about the Holland-Rand family's dark past, hinting at the truth behind Jessica's zombification. They also encourage in her a different way of looking at the world, one rooted in the culture of the colonized rather than the culture of the colonizer. At the urging of one of Fort Holland's maids, Alma (Theresa Harris), Betsy spirits Jessica out of Fort Holland at night midway through the movie and takes her to the voodoo Houmfort in the hope that its priest might be able to cure her zombieism. This pivotal sequence speaks to Betsy's realization that the Western narrative of white racial and cultural superiority may be nothing more than a convenient myth.

Betsy's growing willingness to cross colonial boundaries in the film is suggested by her evolving relationship with the film's black zombie, Carrefour (Darby Jones), who functions not as the symptom of a dead white culture, like Jessica, but as the guardian of a vital black culture. She reacts with fear when she first encounters him stationed on the path to the Houmfort, but the movie's prologue—a scene that takes place after the events of the story, which she narrates in flashback—shows her strolling with him down a sunlit beach. Accompanied by her thoughtful voice-over ("I walked with a zombie" are the first words she speaks), it captures the sort of cultural interaction that Carrefour's name (French for "crossroads") implies, conjuring an older and wiser Betsy who has come to reject the concept of racial Otherness central to Western imperialism, and perhaps even to accept the notion of her own whiteness as a kind of living death.

But *I Walked with a Zombie* is not just about the moral education of its white heroine; it is also about racial justice and reparation for generations of black suffering under the yoke of colonialism on Saint Sebastian. The film's black characters do more than facilitate Betsy's cultural enlightenment; they actively seek redress for their oppression and exploitation by the island's whites. In fact, their quest for restitution becomes the focus of the second half of the movie, after Betsy's visit to the

Houmfort with Jessica reveals that Mrs. Rand, the colony's white matriarch, has not only misappropriated their religion in order to punish her daughter-in-law's petty sexual indiscretions but also masqueraded as the god Damballa in order to manipulate their behavior. Ultimately, they use their influence to precipitate Jessica's murder at the hands of Wesley, who, in a trance-like state, stabs her with an arrow drawn from the figurehead of Ti-Misery and carries her body into the ocean, where he perishes as well.

This white murder-suicide is at once a concrete reprisal for Mrs. Rand's affront to Saint Sebastian's black culture and a symbolic reckoning for the island's history of colonialism in which a souvenir of slavery becomes the instrument of the colonizer's demise. As the climax of the movie, it in many ways eclipses in importance Betsy's moral awakening as the white heroine; indeed, she is essentially absent in the film's final moments. Tourneur and Lewton end instead with a nameless black narrator who solemnly pronounces Jessica "dead in her own life" and "dead in the selfishness of her spirit," a white zombie emblematic of the evils of colonialism. And as Roy Webb's plangent score swells, the camera dollies in to a close-up of Ti-Misery, pierced with arrows and weathered black by time, inviting us to consider, once again, the high cost of Western imperialism.

I Walked with a Zombie is arguably the apex of colonial zombie cinema, but it is far from the only film to follow *White Zombie* in exploring the deathly nature of whiteness. Reginald Le Borg's *Voodoo Island* (1957) stars Boris Karloff as an investigative reporter who learns that the black inhabitants of an island in the South Pacific have resisted Western incursion by zombifying the whites trying to turn their home into a resort for wealthy Americans. In Edward L. Cahn's *Zombies of Mora Tau* (1957), treasure hunters discover that a shipwreck off the coast of Africa is guarded by a crew of white zombies who, having stolen diamonds from a voodoo temple in the late nineteenth century, are doomed to watch over them for all eternity. Even George Marshall's horror-comedy *The Ghost Breakers* (1940), a Bob Hope vehicle, centers on the dreadful legacy of Western imperialism, telling the story of a zombie-haunted castle in Cuba that is inherited by an American woman whose great-grandfather was once the biggest slaveholder on the island. Again and again, in ways both large and small, zombie films from the colonial era prompt viewers to envisage whiteness as a kind of living death.

This is not to say that these films do so with a progressive agenda in mind, necessarily; in truth, some of them could be described as unapologetically racist or imperialist. Victor Halperin's *Revolt of the Zombies* (1936) plays up the "yellow peril" posed by an army of the living dead under the control of Cambodian priests during World War I, for example, while Jean Yarbrough's *King of the Zombies* (1941), ostensibly about an Austrian scientist who uses zombification to steal Allied secrets during World War II, is actually more interested in the subordination of the black comic actor Mantan Moreland, making "the (white) audience's enjoyment of his transformation from 'coon' to zombie . . . [its] chief focus" (Russell 35). But even these movies, by their virulent insistence on white, Western supremacy, encourage reflection on the "white blight" of Western imperialism—especially in a twenty-first-century spectator.

With the end of the colonial era, the number of zombie movies establishing the monster as a creature of voodoo dropped off precipitously. In the second half of the twentieth century, the zombie was essentially deracinated, divorced from its roots in Afro-Caribbean folklore and redefined in the West as a flesh-eating ghoul. As Lauro notes, what had been a clear metaphor for slavery became a "slave metaphor": "usurped, colonized, and altered to represent the struggles of a distinctly different culture" (*Transatlantic* 17). Zombie cinema did not cease at this point to deal with issues of race and racism, however. Indeed, although the folkloric origins of the living dead have played a progressively smaller role in postcolonial zombie movies, they too address racial oppression and exploitation, fixing in particular on the plight of formerly colonized nations and racial minorities in the West under neocolonialism. If colonial zombie cinema captures the heyday of imperialism, when Western powers exerted direct control over the bodies and lands of racial Others, postcolonial zombie cinema portrays its afterlife, as the same powers—now often fronted by multinational corporations with a global reach—have reasserted that control indirectly through cultural and economic means. In both, the focus is ultimately on whites as dead and bringers of death. While postcolonial zombie films frequently feature people of color as the living dead, they leave little doubt who the real zombies are, preserving a space for audiences to contemplate the deathliness of whiteness.

Zombie movies made early in the postcolonial era reflect the revolutionary fervor of the black struggle against white rule during the waning days of Western imperialism in the 1960s and 1970s, when many colonies in the Caribbean—as well as in Africa, Latin America, Asia, and the Middle East—won their independence. Gorier than colonial zombie films, they also paint a far more militant picture of the fight for racial justice and reparation. At the same time, they retain the folkloric origins of the living dead, casting black magic as a source of strength for an insurgent black culture. Set in a world shaped by centuries of white hegemony, where racism is not just endemic but institutionalized, they depict black uprisings in which voodoo is a vehicle for insurrection and the zombie an instrument of revenge. Particularly rich veins of early postcolonial zombie cinema run through blaxploitation horror and Italian horror of the period.

Blaxploitation horror movies appeared in the wake of successful blaxploitation action films like Gordon Parks's *Shaft* (1971) and Jack Hill's *Coffy* (1973), which featured black actors in stories focusing on organized crime in the inner city. Over the course of the 1970s, blaxploitation horror movies reinvented the tropes of white horror to serve African American audiences ignored by Hollywood. Although these horror films, like the action movies that preceded them, were often produced and directed by whites—and have been accused of perpetuating white stereotypes about African Americans—they also imbued the genre with new racial purpose. Reimagining the monster as a figure of black pride and black power, movies like William Crain's *Blacula* (1972) and Bill Gunn's *Ganja and Hess* (1973) shifted audience identification, as Harry M. Benshoff writes, "away from the status quo 'normality' of bourgeois white society" and even worked to expose "white 'normality,' and especially white patriarchy, as productive of monsters" (45).

Paul Maslansky's *Sugar Hill* (1974), an American International Pictures production, is perhaps the most interesting and memorable zombie film of the 1970s blaxploitation horror cycle. It stars Marki Bey as Diana "Sugar" Hill, a black Houston nightclub owner who turns to voodoo for revenge when her boyfriend is beaten to death by henchmen of the white mafia boss Morgan (Robert Quarry). With help from the voodoo queen Mama Maitresse (Zara Cully), she summons Baron Samedi (Don Pedro Colley) and his army of the living dead, who eliminate the murderers one by one, working their way up to Morgan. The film frames Sugar's vendetta not simply as a personal matter but as part of a broader struggle for racial justice. Her machete-wielding "zombie hit men" (as the movie's tagline describes them) are former slaves dressed in rags, their wrists still shackled, while the mob is depicted as a modern plantocracy, maintaining white power and privilege through the ruthless repression of black people.

Sugar herself emerges as an avatar of postcolonial rage who avenges white-on-black violence by turning the American South's legacy of slavery against its present-day beneficiaries. As the movie's theme song, performed by the Motown soul group The Originals, puts it, "Supernatural voodoo woman / Does her thing at night. / Do her wrong / And you won't see the light!" If colonial zombie movies tend to address issues of race and racism in an elliptical fashion, *Sugar Hill*, like other blaxploitation horror movies, tackles them head-on. It illustrates in remarkably stark terms the persistence of white cultural hegemony even after the collapse of Western imperialism, and the necessity of dismantling it through radical black action. Repurposing the zombie as an agent of social change, it makes clear that although its living dead are black, its actual monsters are white.

Curiously, the same is true of zombie movies made in Italy at about the same time. In the decades after World War II, the burgeoning but impoverished Italian horror-film industry largely devoted itself to churning out low-budget pictures inspired by genre hits from abroad. These movies have often been dismissed as little more than cheap knockoffs of far superior horror films. As Kim Newman argues, however, the best are "surprisingly sophisticated mixes of imitation, pastiche, parody, deconstruction, reinterpretation, and operatic inflation" (188). This is the case with many of the Italian zombie movies that flooded theaters following the box-office success of George A. Romero's *Dawn of the Dead* (1978), sporting titles like *Zombie Holocaust* (*Zombi holocaust*, 1980) and *Black Demons* (*Demoni 3*, 1991).

Although Romero's film served as a kind of template for these movies (especially in its liberal use of gore),

they also deviated from it in significant ways—particularly where its story, which centers on survivors of the
zombie apocalypse who take shelter in a shopping mall,
is concerned. Partly inspired, perhaps, by the popularity
of Italian genres like the "mondo" film, which offered a
pseudodocumentary look at the exotic practices of other
cultures, and the cannibal movie, which staged grisly
encounters between white interlopers and indigenous
tribes in South America, they eschewed its Western setting, returning instead to the Afro-Caribbean roots of
zombie cinema. The result was a run of zombie movies
in Italy beginning in the late 1970s that, like the era's blaxploitation zombie films, confronted audiences with a
postcolonial vision of white deathliness.

The first—and in many respects the most trenchant—
of these movies was Lucio Fulci's *Zombie* (*Zombi 2*,
1979). Marketed as a sequel to *Dawn of the Dead*, which
was shown in Italy under the title *Zombi*, it nevertheless
departs radically from its predecessor. It tells the story of
a young woman, Anne Bowles (Tisa Farrow), who seeks
help from the reporter Peter West (Ian McCulloch) after
her father goes missing in the Caribbean; they trace his
whereabouts to the island of Matul, only to find that it has
been overrun by the living dead. The film at its most basic
level is about the return of the colonial repressed. We
learn that the corpses of the island's former colonized—as

well as its former colonizers, including a band of moldering Spanish conquistadors—have been called forth from their graves by voodoo witch doctors and unleashed on its contemporary white inhabitants, who continue to benefit from its dark past as an imperial outpost. Crucially, Fulci primes the audience to identify not with the zombies' victims, whose deaths are fetishized through lingering closeups of Gianetto De Rossi's spectacularly gruesome gore effects, but with the zombies themselves. As they feed on the white islanders who have lived off the black natives for so long, we are repeatedly invited to share their perspective via point-of-view shots that in effect make us one of the living dead.

Ultimately, the film gestures toward what could be called an apocalyptic postcolonialism. As I have written elsewhere, its final scene, in which hordes of zombies enter New York City, "affirms in a postcolonial fashion that the repressed history of colonialism—the all too often unacknowledged fact that our civilization was built on the backs of Others—has the potential to return with sufficient force to destroy all of Western culture, not just its far-flung outposts" (212). Moreover, by once again aligning our point of view with that of the dead, it prompts us to "feel as though we are the ones being called upon to avenge the past injustices suffered by the victims of colonialism," so that "as we shuffle over the Brooklyn Bridge into Manhattan with the rest of the zombies, we can only view the collapse of white culture with satisfaction" (215).

The apocalyptic postcolonialism evoked at the end of Fulci's film has become a hallmark of more recent postcolonial zombie cinema. While the original age of Western imperialism came to an end with the widespread decolonization of the 1960s and 1970s, subsequent decades have seen the persistence of white hegemony in previously colonized regions as well as in the West. No longer purely a matter of military occupation or political control, it is now about cultural and economic domination, often spearheaded by the multinational corporations that increasingly determine the global flow of capital. Such neocolonialism has meant the ongoing exploitation of people of color in emerging nations, which are kept underdeveloped and dependent on the West. It has also meant the continuing oppression of racial minorities in the Western world, where, on a systemic level, white power and privilege remain largely unchanged— as persistent racial disparities in housing and education, employment and income, and incarceration and murder rates in the United States demonstrate.

Some zombie films have been complicit in neocolonialism, peddling its agenda in cinematic form. For example, Wes Craven's *The Serpent and the Rainbow* (1988)—loosely based on a controversial book of the same title by the Harvard ethnobiologist Wade Davis that reads like a neocolonial sequel to *The Magic Island*—once again advocates for Western intervention in Haiti (this time in response to the breakdown of Jean-Claude Duvalier's brutal regime) with its tale of a crusading white scientist who runs afoul of an evil voodoo sorcerer while on the island investigating a pharmacological basis for zombification. Other recent zombie movies, however, can be seen as witting or unwitting critiques of the racial and cultural tyranny perpetuated by modern forms of imperialism. In fact, late postcolonial zombie cinema is defined by its preoccupation with the idea that the West, in its unrelenting subjugation of racial Others at home and abroad, has doomed itself to extinction. It finally imagines nothing less than the end of whiteness.

This apocalyptic postcolonialism suffuses *Land of the Dead* (2005), George A. Romero's long-awaited follow-up to his original living-dead trilogy. Racial conflict plays a role in those earlier films—especially *Night of the Living Dead* (1968), which emphasizes the tension between its black hero and the white characters who also seek refuge inside an isolated farmhouse after the dead begin to rise from their graves—but it is the main focus in *Land of the Dead*, where whites face catastrophic retribution for their neocolonial oppression and exploitation. The movie is set in a fortified city inhabited by survivors of a zombie apocalypse who are strictly segregated by caste. Its villain, Kaufman (Dennis Hopper), the city's architect and dictator, lives in Fiddler's Green, a luxury high-rise apartment building at the center of town, along with the city's uniformly white and well-heeled elite. The rest of the city's residents, its second-class citizens, eke out a living in the streets below. Aside from the movie's disaffected white male hero, Riley (Simon Baker), most are marked as Others by virtue of race, ethnicity, gender, class, or ability, including the Latino Cholo (John Leguizamo), the disabled and deformed Charlie (Robert Joy), the female prostitute Slack (Asia Argento), and the Irish agitator Mulligan (Bruce McFee). Beyond the walls of the metropolis mill the ultimate outsiders, the living dead, whom the townspeople derisively refer to as "stenches."

The city depends for its survival on supply raids carried out by Riley, Cholo, and other underlings in neighboring towns occupied by the zombies. In return, Kaufman offers them protection, as well as distraction in the form of games and vices. Although some, like Cholo, dream of buying their way into Fiddler's Green, membership is closed to them; they are, as Riley puts it, the "wrong kind." *Land of the Dead* evokes the current neocolonial world order, allegorically representing, as John Lutz observes, "America and its relationship to the underdeveloped, exploited nations on the periphery of empire" (122). Like the United States and other Western powers, Kaufman maintains white hegemony by ruthlessly repressing and exploiting both his own people and those outside the borders of his fiefdom.

But Romero is less interested in limning the state of modern imperialism than he is in demonstrating its unsustainable and self-defeating nature. The neocolonial system devised by Kaufman collapses in spectacular fashion when those whom it oppresses and exploits rise up against it. Denied entry into Fiddler's Green, Cholo steals an armored attack vehicle (tellingly nicknamed "Dead Reckoning") and threatens to turn its missiles on the city if Kaufman does not pay him a hefty ransom. In the meantime, the living dead outside the walls begin to organize under the leadership of the black zombie Big Daddy (Eugene Clark), a former gas-station attendant who has developed some semblance of consciousness and, enraged by the slaughter and subjugation of his fellow dead, inspires them to march on the city in revolt.

Although Cholo's attempt at extortion ends in failure, the zombies successfully breach the city's defenses, overrun its streets, and eventually smash their way into Fiddler's Green, where they feast on its privileged white tenants. Fittingly, Kaufman himself is killed by Big Daddy, who, having trapped the villain in his limousine, punches a fuel nozzle through the windshield, fills the car with gasoline, and blows it up. Meanwhile, the film's white hero, Riley, flees with his compatriots in Dead Reckoning, hoping to find sanctuary—and greater egalitarianism— elsewhere. The city is left to the zombies, who, long maligned, misused, and murdered by the living, finally claim their oppressors' domain as the land of the dead. The movie's message could not be clearer: far from guaranteeing the future of white culture, Western neocolonialism in the end assures its destruction.

This is also ultimately the message of *The Dead* (2010), a British film directed—as well as written, photographed, and produced—by brothers Howard and Jon Ford. In many respects, it represents a return to the origins not only of the zombie as a monster but also of the zombie movie as a genre. Largely shot on location in Burkina Faso and Ghana, the picture imagines an outbreak of the living dead occurring in the zombie's ancestral home of West Africa. Its story concerns a white U.S. Air Force flight engineer, Brian Murphy (Rob Freeman), who is the only survivor when a plane evacuating Western personnel from the subcontinent crashes shortly after takeoff; stranded and utterly outnumbered by the dead, he joins forces with an African army officer, Daniel Dembele (Prince David Oseia), who is making his way to a distant military base in the hope that his missing son has been taken there.

Unfortunately, in retracing the zombie's roots, *The Dead* also recalls the racist and imperialist discourse that gave rise to zombie cinema in the waning days of colonialism. Despite its African setting, it privileges a white, Western perspective, clearly positioning Murphy as the hero. In contrast, Daniel plays little more than a supporting role. Like the faithful black retainers in jungle adventure films from the classical Hollywood era, he acts as Murphy's guide and saves his life several times during their journey before perishing at the hands of the living dead. The dead themselves—who are almost without exception black Africans—serve, like latter-day cannibals, to link racial Otherness with monstrosity, suggesting that it is something to be contained or exterminated. Indeed, the movie revels in the spectacle of black death and dismemberment, dwelling in detail on images of Africans being shot, eaten, hacked to pieces, run over, and torn limb from limb. And its depiction of Africa as the source of a zombie outbreak plays into contemporary Western stereotypes about the continent as a zone of perpetual civil war and genocide and the incubator of deadly diseases like AIDS and Ebola. In these ways and others, *The Dead* feels like a colonialist throwback—an apologia for white intervention in "darkest Africa."

At the same time, like other zombie films from *White Zombie* onward, *The Dead* works to undercut the notion of white racial and cultural superiority, offering, possibly in spite of itself, a sharp critique of Western imperialism. To begin with, the movie implies that white culture, not black magic, is responsible for the outbreak of the living dead in Africa. The exact cause is never revealed, but a tribal leader (David Dontoh) who provides shelter for Murphy and Daniel at one point speculates, "Maybe we're being punished for our arrogance. Perhaps nature has put in motion the ultimate solution to its problem. Man's greed has devoured this earth. Nature is restoring its delicate balance." Although the leader's "we" is inclusive, it's not difficult to read his commentary as an indictment of *white* greed and arrogance; after all, if Africa's natural resources have long been plundered for profit, that plunder began with Western imperialism—and continues today largely under the aegis of neocolonialism. It is interesting that the film's few white zombies include Christian missionaries whom Murphy finds quarantined in an empty village, evidently because they were spreading more than God's word among its inhabitants. And it seems significant that when the movie's black zombies "turn," they develop pale-blue eyes the same color as the white hero's.

One could argue that while *The Dead* reaffirms the stereotype of Africa as a hotbed of disease on one level, it hints on another that the real threat of infection is posed by the West and that the virus is whiteness. Intentionally or not, it conjures the nightmarish vision of a continent in the grip of a colonialism that is officially over but, zombie-like, refuses to die. Moreover, the film insinuates that Western culture, in continuing its depredation in Africa, has condemned itself to living death. At the movie's conclusion, Murphy, having finally made his way to the African military base, uses its radio to contact an Air Force command center in Nevada—only to find that the zombie apocalypse has reached America, where it has toppled the government and taken his family. Digesting this news in stunned silence, he gives the impression of being the last white man on the planet, left to contemplate the massive wave of reverse colonization that has swept away much of the West.

It is undeniably the case that contemporary zombie movies rarely reference the monster's Afro-Caribbean roots. Living death, once a metaphor for slavery, has become, to quote Lauro, something of a slave metaphor, "forced to labor in cinema, carrying the psychic load of a formerly imperialist culture" (*Transatlantic* 9). But as she eloquently notes, "The zombie refuses to be a palimpsest: its history bleeds through our attempts to write over it, and the trace is visible, like ghost graffiti coming through the whitewash" (*Transatlantic* 192), revealing the extent to which "the history of the transatlantic slave trade is still very much a part of everyday life in the United States, the way we might say slavery 'haunts' our cultural conscious-ness" (*Transatlantic* 18). Films like *Land of the Dead* and *The Dead* demonstrate that zombie cinema still grapples with issues of race and racism, often capturing the death-liness of whiteness in much the same manner as movies from the colonial era.

This is not to say, of course that these texts collectively signify "a deeply embedded cultural regret regarding the triangle trade," as opposed to "an unfortunate impulse to repeat the past sins of empires in the form of cultural conquest" (Lauro, *Transatlantic* 9). Zombie cinema has surely been driven by both impulses, as well as others. It is clear, however, that the films discussed in this chapter at the very least provide a space for audiences to think about whites as dead and bringers of death. They represent one crucial way in which the West has been able—even forced—to confront its zombification. If the transforma-tion of the folkloric zombie into a horror-movie monster constitutes an act of cultural appropriation, then, it is also, "like something out of a horror movie, a curse that follows the oppressor home" (Lauro, *Transatlantic* 25).

2

CONSUMER CULTURE

Night of the Living Dead (1968), George A. Romero's supremely bleak film about a small band of survivors trapped in an isolated farmhouse when radiation from space reanimates the dead and sends them shambling through the countryside, occupies a pivotal place in the history of zombie cinema. Shot in stark black and white on a shoestring budget in the hinterlands of western Pennsylvania, it met with little fanfare upon its initial theatrical release but went on to become a cult sensation that revolutionized the zombie film. On that much, critics agree. But revolutionized how?

Night of the Living Dead is frequently cited as the movie that modernized the zombie by severing its ties to Afro-Caribbean folklore. A number of earlier films had already jettisoned the zombie's folkloric origins, however, including Michael Curtiz's *The Walking Dead* (1936), which stars Boris Karloff as a wrongfully executed man who returns from the dead to seek revenge on the gangsters who framed him; and Steve Sekely's *Revenge of the Zombies* (1943), Z-grade program filler from the "poverty row" studio Monogram Pictures about an army of zombies created by a Nazi scientist to fight for the Third Reich. *Night of the Living Dead* is also often cited as the movie that introduced the idea of a zombie apocalypse. Here too, though, it was preceded by films like Edward L. Cahn's *Invisible Invaders* (1959), which imagines the world being invaded by invisible aliens who attack by inhabiting the bodies of the recently deceased; and Ubaldo Ragona and Sidney Salkow's *The Last Man on Earth* (*L'ultimo uomo della Terra*, 1964), an adaptation of Richard Matheson's 1954 novel *I Am Legend* featuring Vincent Price as the only person left alive after a plague turns the rest of humanity into a race of vampire-like zombies.

In fact, Romero's real innovation in *Night of the Living Dead* is his reinvention of the zombie as a flesh-eating ghoul. From its famous opening scene, the movie hints that its living dead are not the stolid, tractable monsters audiences had come to expect from past zombie films. The ghoul that goes after Barbra (Judith O'Dea) and her brother Johnny (Russell Streiner) in the cemetery seems driven by desperate, predatory need, clawing at Barbra when she crosses its path and braining Johnny on a headstone when he intervenes. After Barbra finds refuge in the farmhouse with Ben (Duane Jones) and the other survivors, we learn that the young daughter of the middle-aged couple Harry and Helen Cooper (Karl Hardman and Marilyn Eastman) has been bitten by a zombie. Finally, a TV news bulletin reveals the horrible truth: the dead are killing *and eating* the living. They are not soulless slaves of voodoo or robotic victims of alien mind control but reanimated corpses with a voracious appetite for human flesh—an appetite that the film goes on to document in gruesome detail.

Following a disastrous escape attempt, teenagers Tom (Keith Wayne) and Judy (Judith Ridley) are greedily devoured by the dead, who are shown gnawing on severed limbs, tearing meat from bones, and fighting over ropes of intestine. And in the movie's most iconic scene, the Coopers' little girl, Karen (Kyra Schon), having succumbed to her bite, cannibalizes her parents as the zombies outside mount their climactic assault on the farmhouse. The shocking notion that the dead might desire to feed on the living was unprecedented and proved hugely influential. At a stroke, Romero's film irrevocably altered the nature of the zombie as a monster. But that wasn't its only contribution to zombie cinema. In redefining the dead—quite literally—as consumers, it introduced what became one of the modern zombie movie's dominant metaphors: living death as an analogue for late-stage capitalism.

Of course, the link between capitalism and living death had been established in zombie cinema long before *Night of the Living Dead*. Indeed, pointing to the fact that the birth of the zombie film coincided with the Great Depression, critics have argued that the genre was inspired as much by capitalism as it was by colonialism. The image of the mindless zombie drone resonated with audiences suffering through the worst economic crisis of the twentieth century. As David J. Skal writes, the "shuffling spectacle of the walking dead in films like *White Zombie* (1932) was in many ways a nightmare vision of a breadline" for viewers who "knew that they were no longer completely in control of their lives; the economic strings were being pulled by faceless, frightening forces" (168–169). The blank-eyed zombie served as a potent metaphor for "an economic zombification of terrifying proportions" (Russell 23).

A "dead worker resurrected as a slave into a hellish afterlife of endless toil," the zombie also perfectly captured life under industrial capitalism, laying bare the "dark side of capitalist economics" that reduced human beings to "expendable automatons" (Russell 23). It spoke to how the factory assembly line, powered by the principles of standardization, mechanization, mass production, and scientific management, had transformed labor into a kind of living death during the first half of the twentieth century. Well after the Depression ended, the zombie continued to operate as a cinematic stand-in for the exploited and dehumanized wage slave in Western capitalist society. For example, in John Gilling's *The Plague of the Zombies* (1966), a British picture from Hammer Films, the dead in a nineteenth-century Cornish village are pressed into service by a local squire who runs his tin mine like a zombie sweatshop. By the late 1960s, zombies had functioned in film for some time as "capitalist monsters": creatures who "embody the contradictions of a culture where making a living often feels like dying" (Newitz 2).

But in *Night of the Living Dead*, the zombie emerges as a new breed of capitalist monster, one reflecting the nature of late-stage capitalism. If earlier representations of the dead capture the plight of the worker under industrial capitalism, the flesh-eating ghouls of Romero's film herald the rise of an economy rooted not in the manufacture of goods but in the consumption of them. Its shocking, unprecedented scenes of zombie cannibalism symbolically describe life under the postindustrial capitalism that developed during the second half of the twentieth century, fueled by the emergence of globalized markets and labor, multinational corporations, mass media, and the service industry. As Christopher Sharrett notes, *Night of the Living Dead* was the "first work to literalize the theme of cannibalism . . . [as] the image of society feeding on itself" (311). In it, Romero returns to the "man-eating myth," once used as a justification for Western imperialism and colonialism, and reveals it to be "a story about *ourselves*, not others" (Kilgour 247)—the ideal metaphor for the unbridled consumerism that defines the dominant culture in the West today. In doing so, he transformed zombie cinema into a space for us to contemplate what Crystal Bartolovich, playfully repurposing Fredric Jameson's work on postmodernism and late capitalism, calls the cultural logic of late cannibalism.

This chapter explores the ways in which zombie films made since *Night of the Living Dead* depict contemporary capitalism as a kind of living death, framing cannibalism not only as a trope for a society propelled by the "desire for infinite (capitalist) consumption" but also as "one of the morbid symptoms of capitalist appetite in crisis" (Bartolovich 232, 234)—a sign that, thanks to the effects of both rampant overaccumulation and endemic economic disparity, we are rapidly approaching capitalism's apocalyptic limit. As Gwendolyn Audrey Foster observes, we "consume recklessly in order to convince ourselves that we are not alienated, and that late-stage capitalism will provide for us, and fulfill our emotional needs" (*Hoarders* 28). In the end, however, we are ourselves consumed by the capitalist appetite that drives us. This, ultimately, is the message of the films I consider in the pages that follow.

If *Night of the Living Dead* introduced the idea of the flesh-eating ghoul as the quintessential late-capitalist consumer, Romero's sequel, *Dawn of the Dead* (1978), memorably cemented the metaphor by turning its zombies into shoppers—and its shoppers into zombies. Opening in the midst of a chaotic zombie outbreak in Philadelphia, *Dawn of the Dead* follows the fortunes of the television-station employees Fran (Gaylen Ross) and Stephen (David Emge), who, along with the SWAT team officers Peter (Ken Foree) and Roger (Scott H. Reiniger), flee the city in a helicopter. They eventually find shelter at the Monroeville Mall, a gigantic indoor shopping complex near Pittsburgh. From the moment of their arrival, the movie establishes a connection between capitalism and living death.

Romero, who shot the picture largely on location in the Monroeville Mall, filming after hours over the holiday shopping season in 1977, frames the complex as a capitalist mecca, a temple to consumerism complete with department stores, restaurants, hair salons, video game arcades, gun retailers, banks—even an ice-skating rink. As the heroes notice when they land on its roof, it is completely surrounded by the dead, who seem eager to get in. "Why do they come here?" a bewildered Fran asks. "Some kind of instinct. Memory. What they used to do. This was an important place in their lives," Stephen responds. The social commentary here, noted by many critics over the years, is difficult to miss: the zombies represent the kind of mindless consumers produced by late-capitalist culture. The dead who have managed to gain entry to the mall behave just like the living, wandering its polished floors, window shopping, and riding the escalators as Muzak plays over the PA system. When Peter and Roger raid the J. C. Penney's for supplies, the dead mob the locked glass doors like bargain hunters on Black Friday waiting impatiently for the store to open. The zombie apocalypse may have occurred, but at the Monroeville Mall, it's business as usual.

Indeed, Romero suggests that the zombies aren't the only shoppers in the mall. Although survival is the priority for Fran, Stephen, Peter, and Roger when they first arrive, they are soon seduced by the possibilities the place offers for mass consumption: "One-stop shopping," as Roger puts it. "Everything you need, right at your fingertips." Once they rid the mall of its roaming dead and barricade its doors against intruders, they go on an extended spree, withdrawing money from the bank, donning expensive clothes and jewelry, gorging on gourmet cheeses and coffee, and playing video games—all for free. Their shopper's high doesn't last long, however. As Tony Williams notes, the mall, an "affluent symbol of capitalist consumption, . . . eventually contaminates them," effectively transforming them into zombies (151). Their gluttony has an anesthetizing effect; they become increasingly bored and prone to bickering. "What have we done to ourselves?" Fran wonders plaintively. The answer is clear. Uninhibited consumerism has made them something less than human. Peter speaks to this in a key exchange with Fran, as they idly watch the zombies massed outside the mall, still clamoring to get in. "What the hell are they?" she asks. He replies, "They're us—that's all."

The extent of the heroes' zombification is revealed at the movie's climax, when a violent biker gang invades the shopping center. Despite the fact that the luxury goods the mall houses have little use-value in a postapocalyptic world, the heroes are determined to defend it. As Stephen insists, "It's ours. We took it. It's ours!" The anarchy that ensues ultimately serves only to deliver the mall back into the hands of the dead, who actually prove to be less materialistic than the living. To the tune of Herbert Chappell's "The Gonk," a sprightly polka number, the dead shuffle obliviously through piles of paper money, knock over shopping displays, and break expensive bottles of perfume. Although Peter and Fran manage to escape in the helicopter at the end, their survival is an open question—not just because they are low on fuel but because they have been unable to break the hold that late capitalism has on them. Viewers today, taken aback by Romero's

Brechtian use of satirical humor and the special-effects wizard Tom Savini's cartoonish gore, often find the film dated, but its message about the deadening effect of mass consumption is more relevant now than ever.

The impact of *Dawn of the Dead* on zombie cinema has been as lasting as that of *Night of the Living Dead*. While Zack Snyder's 2004 remake eschews social commentary in favor of high-octane action, Romero's movie has inspired a number of contemporary zombie films, from Edgar Wright's *Shaun of the Dead* (2004), whose British hero is so numbed by life under late capitalism that he fails to notice at first that the dead are returning to life, to Alejandro Brugués's *Juan of the Dead* (*Juan de los muertos*, 2011), whose Cuban protagonist, bitten by the capitalist bug, is as rapacious as the dead in his efforts to cash in on the zombie apocalypse. But compulsive consumerism is not the only type of capitalist consumption critiqued in modern zombie cinema.

Cannibalism also figures as a metaphor for the West's relentless consumption of natural resources in movies featuring what Sarah Juliet Lauro calls the "eco-zombie": a monster that "channels contemporary characterizations of a planet angered by humanity's long-term damage" by embodying nature's "retaliation for humanity's abuse of its environment" ("Eco-Zombie" 55). The eco-zombie first emerged in Europe during the 1970s, a time when new concerns about industrial capitalism's impact on the planet—in the form of acid rain, toxic waste, pollution, and deforestation—gave birth to the modern environmentalist movement. Russ Hunter has written about how Italian zombie pictures such as Umberto Lenzi's *Nightmare City* (*Incubo sulla città contaminata*, 1980) and Bruno Mattei's *Hell of the Living Dead* (*Virus*, 1980) engage "with some of the concerns of the deeper ecological movement that began to gain momentum in the latter half of the 1970s," offering a "cautionary representation of the power of man to change and (mis)manage the ecosystem" (114, 128). A similar engagement is evident in the French zombie films of Jean Rollin, whose *The Grapes of Death* (*Les raisins de la mort*, 1978) and *The Living Dead Girl* (*La morte vivante*, 1982) present living death as a symbol and symptom of environmental destruction under late capitalism.

This cycle of European eco-zombie cinema was launched by Jorge Grau's seminal *Let Sleeping Corpses Lie* (*Non si deve profanare il sonno dei morte*, 1974). An Italian production shot largely on location in England by a Spanish filmmaker, it concerns a young antiques dealer, George (Ray Lovelock), who goes on holiday, leaving his shop in Manchester to visit friends in the Lake District. On the way, his motorcycle is damaged in a fender bender with Edna (Cristina Galbó), who offers him the use of her car if he'll accompany her to her sister's home in South

Gate. There, he is caught up in a series of strange local murders that turn out to be the work of zombies reanimated by an agricultural experiment gone awry.

Grau wastes no time in establishing the environmentalist themes of the movie. Ironically opening on the statue of a fertility goddess—one of several pieces George plans to deliver to his friends in Windermere—he cuts to a credits sequence exhibiting images from the hellish urban industrial landscape that his hero traverses on the way out of Manchester: belching smokestacks, billowing tailpipes, pedestrians in face masks, a dead bird on the pavement. The lush green countryside seems to hold out the promise of escape and renewal but has itself been fatally compromised by human activity. George's investigation into the murders in South Gate reveals that the dead are being revived as bloodthirsty cannibals by a device designed by the Ministry of Agriculture to eradicate farm pests using ultrasonic radiation. Significantly, no one in a position of authority—neither the government scientists nor the town's bigoted police inspector nor the local hospital's head physician—believes him. Indeed, the machine's range of operation is expanded, sealing George and Edna's fate and throwing South Gate's future into question. Grau depicts a society doomed by its reckless attempts to exploit and control nature, setting the stage for the European eco-zombie movies that followed, as well as for later films like Dan O'Bannon's cheerfully nihilistic *The Return of the Living Dead* (1985) and Carl Bessai's more recent *Severed* (2005), both of which deal with environmental apocalypses.

Twenty-first-century zombie pictures have also employed the trope of cannibalism as a means of capturing our appetite for the definitive product of the late-capitalist era: mass media. The French theorist Guy Debord describes Western culture under late capitalism as a society of the spectacle—a realm in which capital has "accumulated to the point where it becomes image," creating a "social relationship between people that is mediated by images" (24, 12). As all that "was directly lived has become mere representation" (Debord 12)—a simulation substituting, in the words of Jean Baudrillard, "the signs of the real for the real" (2)—the focus of our consumption has become the signifiers for things rather than things themselves. This is especially true in the new millennium, thanks to the digital revolution, the arrival of the internet, and the rise of social media, which have helped to shape an economy whose chief currency is images and whose most highly prized commodity is information.

Cinema itself, unmoored from its material basis in celluloid film, has become just another article of trade in the digital domain, an audiovisual service, as Wheeler Winston Dixon observes, "in a streaming world where everything . . . [is] available like running water—all you have to do is pay the utility bill" (24). At the same time, movies have played a vital role in maintaining the contemporary society of the spectacle. This is a key focus of recent "media zombie" movies that self-reflexively critique the ghoulish way in which images are produced and consumed under capitalism today. Zombie mockumentaries like Grace Lee's *American Zombie* (2007) draw on and subvert the documentary form to implicate both the filmmaker and the viewer as late-stage cannibals; a similar approach is taken in found-footage zombie films like Jaume Balagueró and Paco Plaza's *[Rec]* (2007). Exploring the idea of "media as an infective medium" (Dyson 138), they illustrate Baudrillard's dictum that "we live in a world where there is more and more information and less and less meaning" (79).

The "zombie doc" that offers perhaps the most trenchant analysis of the connection between mass media and living death is George A. Romero's *Diary of the Dead* (2007). Building on the critique of the media in *Night of the Living Dead* and *Dawn of the Dead*, both of which skewer television as an instrument of misinformation and manipulation, *Diary of the Dead* uses the conceit of the found-footage horror film to demonstrate how filmmakers and audiences "collaborate together in the mutual project of cannibalizing living subjects in order to turn them into the living dead" (Laist 104). The movie presents itself as the digital diary of a group of University of Pittsburgh film students who, when a zombie outbreak interrupts their work on a class project, set out to document the apocalypse. Especially gung-ho is the director, Jason (Josh Close), who is determined to capture the whole thing on camera and upload it for viewers online. In contrast, his girlfriend, Debra (Michelle Morgan)—who has compiled the footage for us and serves as its cautionary narrator—worries that their diary is slowly dehumanizing them.

The film bears out Debra's concern. Romero frames Jason's compulsion to chronicle the apocalypse as a ghastly cannibalization of reality. Perpetually shooting, a metaphorical act of violence likened to gunplay on several occasions, he feeds on the living in much the same way the dead do. In particular, his willingness to dispassionately record his friends' moments of grief and terror—even their deaths—marks him as a media zombie. And like a zombie, he is contagious: his need to film spreads like an infection. Even Debra is not immune, as we see at the end of the movie when she records Jason's death after he is bitten by a zombie and then insists on finishing the diary he started. But as she muses at one point in voice-over, "the shooters" are not solely responsible for the infectious spread of media; viewers are just as accountable. It is ultimately their hunger for Jason's work online—a rough cut of his footage gets seventy-two thousand hits in eight minutes on the web—that causes it to "go viral." If we now inhabit a world in which reality has become indistinguishable from simulation, in which the truth has been replaced by information, Romero suggests that we're all to blame. Under late capitalism, everybody is a media zombie.

Images are not the only mechanism of infection explored in media zombie cinema, however. The Canadian filmmaker Bruce McDonald's *Pontypool* (2008), one of the most innovative zombie pictures of the past decade, focuses on the viral nature of language. Loosely based on Tony Burgess's 1995 novel *Pontypool Changes Everything*, it tells the story of the "shock jock" DJ Grant Mazzy (Stephen McHattie), who, along with his producer, Sydney Briar (Lisa Houle), and her assistant, Laurel-Ann Drummond (Georgina Reilly), is trapped in a radio station after a zombie outbreak occurs in the small town of Pontypool, Ontario. The epidemic is the result of a linguistic virus that spreads when words it has infected are spoken to and understood by a living host, who becomes a zombie compelled to repeat the word, passing the disease on to others. The dead hunt for victims in cannibalistic packs, chanting contagiously; eventually, they converge on the radio station, attracted by Mazzy's broadcast.

The film can be read as a pointed allegory about the virulent effect of mass media—especially the kind of inflammatory discourse associated with talk radio. Exploring the influence that irreverent, aggressive on-air personalities like Howard Stern and Don Imus have on their audience, McDonald imagines his protagonist as a vector for actual disease. A self-styled cowboy whose credo is "taking no prisoners" and whose aim is provocation rather than communication, Mazzy has made a career out of inciting outrage among his listeners; now, his "hot talk" has literally created a hot zone. While it's not clear that he's the source of the media virus, the movie leaves no doubt that his decision to stay on the air and report on the outbreak facilitates its unchecked replication. The only defense against it, as he and Sydney finally discover, is to deconstruct language—to divorce words from their meaning— or to switch to a different tongue (in a canny comment on linguistic imperialism, McDonald makes English the only infected language). Their realization comes too late. In a bid to stop the spread of the virus, the military bombs the radio station, killing them both. But the damage has already been done: as the credits roll, we hear the disease sweep across the airwaves, multiplying exponentially in yet another testament to the deadening effect of mass media.

Released exactly forty years after *Night of the Living Dead*, *Pontypool* demonstrates once again the enduring influence of Romero's film. Like all of the movies discussed so far in this chapter, it frames the zombie as a cannibal, linking living death with consumption under late capitalism. There are recent zombie films, though, that have updated its conception of the monster to better reflect the condition of capitalist culture in the West today. In these movies, the dead figure not as consumers, primarily, but as consumed—as monsters hollowed out and driven mad by the insatiable hunger symptomatic of their condition. They evoke the way in which capitalism seems to have now reached a terminal stage. As a system, it has proven increasingly precarious in the twenty-first century, prone to ever-larger booms and busts as markets balloon, inflated by the irrational exuberance of investors, only to implode in spectacular fashion. Financial meltdowns like the one that occurred in 2008, triggered by predatory lending practices in the housing sector and the unregulated trade of collateralized debt obligations by banks "too big to fail," now threaten the entire economy. Meanwhile, the divide between the "haves" and the "have-nots" has never been wider, with the wealthiest 1 percent controlling the vast majority of the world's resources while the other 99 percent compete for the remaining sliver of the pie. Subsistence under late capitalism today is either feast or famine, fueling widespread protest and social unrest. This state of affairs is captured in the current crop of zombie movies by the emergence of a new kind of ghoul. Variously known as the fast zombie, the rage zombie, or the plague zombie, it invites us to contemplate our place in an economy that has spiraled out of control and appears to be on the verge of consuming itself.

The film that popularized this new strain of living death is Danny Boyle's *28 Days Later* (2002). Inspired in part by John Wyndham's 1951 "cosy catastrophe" novel *The Day of the Triffids*, adapted for the screen in 1963 by Steve Sekely and an uncredited Freddie Francis, it stars Cillian Murphy as Jim, a bicycle courier who awakens from a coma in the hospital to discover that England has been ravaged by the accidental release of a bioengineered "rage" virus that transforms its victims into violent, frenzied zombies. The "infected," as they're called in the movie, are often read as Others embodying millennial anxieties about terrorism and pandemics, but Boyle has emphasized in interviews that "it's not a film about monsters—it's a film about us!" (Charity 72). In particular, he says, he and the screenwriter, Alex Garland, were interested in commenting on our predisposition to rage as twenty-first-century consumers: "Air rage, parking rage, trolley rage in the supermarkets. [We thought] what if we could employ *that* as the element that constitutes the zombies?" (Morrison 100). As Jamie Russell notes, the picture "suggests that anger—'rage' itself—has become the defining emotional response in late capitalist societies" (135). Although the film's grainy digital images of a devastated and depopulated London eerily prefigure news footage from the aftermath of 9/11 (which occurred during its production), and its narrative focus on the global spread of a deadly disease seems to address in advance the SARS outbreak that followed its release, it's chiefly a movie not about the monsters outside our borders but about the monster already inside us. Conceived at a time of economic uncertainty and malaise, in the wake of the troubled launch of the euro in 1999 and the dot-com collapse in 2000, its zombies conjure "the increasingly desperate hyper-consumers of terminal credit-based capitalism" (Drake 230). *28 Days Later* chronicles the uncontrollable, infectious anger of a capitalist society teetering on the edge of apocalypse.

The film can also be construed as a plea for us to step back from the brink, a cautionary tale about the consequences of surrendering to late capitalism's culture of rage. Symbolically reborn in the movie's opening moments, awaking naked and alone in a London hospital, Jim is delivered into a new world in which two possible modes of survival are open to him: one, communal and cooperative; the other, autonomous and competitive. It quickly becomes clear that he prefers collaboration. When he is rescued from the infected by two fellow survivors, Mark (Noah Huntley) and Selena (Naomie Harris), he throws in with them at once. He soon discovers, however, that their partnership is one of convenience only. When Mark is bitten by a zombie shortly after Jim joins them, the fiercely independent Selena dispatches him without hesitation and promises to do the same to Jim if he becomes infected. His arguments against her ruthlessly Darwinian, dog-eat-dog outlook—a sad remnant of capitalism, like the worthless pound notes drifting through the streets and the unhealthy junk food on which they subsist—initially fall on deaf ears. It is not until they team up with the former cabbie Frank (Brendan Gleeson) and his teenage daughter, Hannah (Megan Burns), who have intercepted a radio broadcast from a military base in Manchester promising an "answer to infection," that he persuades her of the value of close collaboration and personal relationships to survival. As the four of them head north toward the source of the transmission, they gradually become something of an informal family.

But Jim's faith in cooperation as an alternative to competition is put to the test when they finally arrive at their destination. Tragically, they lose father figure Frank to the infection; worse, they learn that the radio recording is a trap designed to lure survivors to a country manor fortified by a detachment of soldiers whose commander, Major West (Christopher Eccleston), has kept up his men's morale by promising them women. West himself makes no distinction between preapocalyptic and post-apocalyptic existence; as he tells his new "guests," he's seen the same thing in the four weeks since infection that he saw in the four weeks before that: "people killing people." In his view, life is purely a question of the survival of the fittest. His attempt to maintain a sense of domestic "normalcy" at the manor despite the chaos surrounding it marks him as a diehard adherent of end-stage capitalism. Indeed, Boyle draws an explicit parallel between the soldiers and the zombies they battle: they keep one of their number, a black private named Mailer (Marvin Campbell) who has been infected with the rage virus, chained in the courtyard for study—a nod to George A. Romero's *Day of the Dead* (1985), which revolves in part around the training of a zombie test subject held in an underground military installation. Jim protests when he discovers West's plans for Selena and Hannah, but to little effect. The women are simply claimed as commodities and prepared for a life of sexual slavery, while he is marched into the woods for a summary execution. Miraculously, he is able to escape, and it is here that his character takes an interesting turn.

Jim drops the philosophy of survival he adopted at the beginning of the film, returns to the manor under the cover of darkness, frees Mailer, and joins the zombie on a bloody rampage through the compound, savagely killing the soldiers he comes across. He is now the one linked with living death; in fact, when he rescues Selena from rape at the hands of the sadistic Corporal Mitchell (Ricci Harnett) by murdering the officer with his bare hands, she briefly believes that he has been infected by the virus. Figuratively speaking, he has been: tainted by the soldiers' continued allegiance to a capitalist system defined by its disregard for the lives and rights of others, he has become something less than human. And in the film's original ending (altered for its theatrical run but made available in its release on DVD and Blu-Ray as a supplement to the movie), he pays for it with his life. Shot by West as he makes his escape from the manor with Selena and Hannah, he dies on an operating table in a hospital very much like the one he awoke in at the beginning of the movie, bearing out Friedrich Nietzsche's warning that he who fights with monsters "should look to it that he himself does not become a monster" (68). When you gaze into the abyss of late capitalism, Boyle seems to be saying, it also gazes into you.

28 Days Later was not the first movie to feature rage zombies. Romero pioneered the concept in *The Crazies* (1973), a film about a small town in Pennsylvania whose inhabitants are transformed into homicidal maniacs by a biological weapon that is accidentally released into the municipal water supply by the military, and it subsequently served as a means of exploring the bestial-izing effects of war on American soldiers returning from Vietnam in pictures like Bob Clark's *Deathdream* (1974) and Antonio Margheriti's *Cannibal Apocalypse* (*Apoc-alypse domani*, 1980). Boyle's movie was, however, the first to make the rage zombie an emblem of late capital-ism, introducing a figure that has inspired a wide range of films, from Juan Carlos Fresnadillo's sequel, *28 Weeks Later* (2007), which chronicles the inevitable spread of the rage virus from England to the European continent, to Tommy Wirkola's *Dead Snow* (*Død snø*, 2009), which focuses on Nazi zombies in the mountains of Norway who rabidly guard a cache of looted treasure from all out-siders (an apt metaphor for the reemergence of far-right nationalist parties running on anti-immigrant platforms across Europe over the past decade). But perhaps the most interesting—and certainly the most surprising—recent zombie pictures to examine rage as a symptom of late capitalism are a series of Hollywood blockbusters that despite being model late-capitalist products themselves nevertheless expose, intentionally or not, the way in which consumers have become the consumed in today's apocalyptic economy.

Such is the case with the first true zombie blockbuster: Francis Lawrence's *I Am Legend* (2007), a $150 million adaptation of Richard Matheson's novel bankrolled by

Warner Bros. with the Hollywood star Will Smith in the lead. Smith plays Robert Neville, a military scientist working in New York City to find the cure for a plague to which he is immune but which three years earlier decimated the planet's population and turned most of the survivors into "Dark Seekers": frenzied, bloodthirsty zombies who sleep during the day and hunt in packs at night. Not surprisingly, given that the film's postapocalyptic vision of Manhattan as "ground zero" for a global pandemic deliberately evokes 9/11 and the bunker mentality of the Bush-Cheney years, *I Am Legend* has often been read by critics as a "neocon fantasy" (Russell 202).

On a deeper level, though, the movie functions as a remarkably incisive—and prophetic—parable of economic resentment and class warfare under late capitalism. Neville, apparently the last human in New York City, represents the world economy's privileged few. By day, he tools around the overgrown streets of midtown Manhattan in a sports car, shopping for music at Tower Records, hitting golf balls off the deck of the USS *Intrepid*, and hunting game in Times Square with his sole companion, a German shepherd named Sam. By night, he beds down in a palatial townhouse on Washington Square Park—the same home he occupied with his wife and child, who are now dead, before the outbreak of the plague—listening to Bob Marley on his iPod and living off of his huge stockpile of food, surrounded by priceless paintings from the Museum of Modern Art. Meanwhile, the Dark Seekers represent the underprivileged masses, squatting in dank warehouses and abandoned office buildings, subsisting on little more than their hatred for Neville, whose base of operations they spend every night trying to locate and destroy. As Jamie Russell notes, although the "movie predates the Occupy Wall Street movement, . . . it anticipates the battle between the haves and have-nots fought on the streets of Manhattan a few years later" (201).

Interestingly, the film's sympathies—like those of Matheson's novel—seem to lie not with Neville, whom it depicts as somewhat less than human, but with the zombies, whom it reveals to be something more than monsters. While Neville regards the Dark Seekers as little better than animals, disposable test subjects he traps and experiments on in his quest to develop a vaccine for the plague, it becomes obvious that they retain much of their humanity—possibly more than he does. They demonstrate a keen intelligence, at one point detaining him in the open past nightfall with the same kind of snare he has been using to catch them. More importantly, they live communally and cultivate strong bonds, as is clear from the anguished reaction of their leader, the Alpha Male (Dash Mihok), when Neville captures his mate, the Alpha Female (Joanna Numata).

Neville, on the other hand, is defined—and dehumanized—by his solitude and aloofness. He prefers to interact with department-store dummies he has nicknamed and placed around town (though he can't bring himself to speak to one female mannequin that serves as his imaginary "love interest"). When he has the opportunity to connect with two other human survivors, Anna (Alice Braga) and Ethan (Charlie Tahan), a Brazilian aid worker and a young boy who respond to his radio broadcasts, he proves spectacularly inept, parroting dialogue from the animated children's film *Shrek* (2001)—which he has evidently memorized—in a sad attempt at communication. "You're not so good with people anymore, are you?" Anna observes. Most damningly, Neville refuses to accept the new world order and cede "his" city to the Dark Seekers. When the zombies finally track him down and smash their way into his townhouse, he opts to blow up himself—and them—rather than allow the underclass to take over. Although a tacked-on happy ending shows Anna and Ethan escaping the city with Neville's newly discovered cure for the plague, *I Am Legend* ultimately offers an apocalyptic view of late capitalism, one in which the vast economic divide between the 1 percent and the 99 percent essentially assures their mutual destruction.

Another side of apocalyptic capitalism is examined in Breck Eisner's *The Crazies* (2010), an intelligent remake of Romero's 1973 movie produced under the banner of Participant Media, a company dedicated to entertainment that inspires social change. In this film, the focus is on the slow death of small-town America—particularly farming communities in the Midwest—under the post-industrial economy of the new millennium. Set in the rural hamlet of Ogden Marsh, Iowa, it follows the efforts of the local sheriff, David Dutton (Timothy Olyphant), to cope with a zombie outbreak caused by a biological agent introduced into the town's water supply after a military transport plane carrying it crashes in a nearby swamp. Designed by the government to "destabilize" an enemy population in warfare, the virus, code-named Trixie, drives those who are exposed to it into a murderous rage, turning them against their friends and families. As it sweeps rapidly through the community, Dutton has to contend not only with the violent "crazies" it creates but also with the trigger-happy troops sent in to stop its spread by any means necessary.

The film's interest lies in its suggestion that the real apocalypse hit long before this zombie outbreak—that Trixie is merely amplifying the anger, hopelessness, and desperation of small-town Americans who feel left behind in the late-capitalist era. Tellingly, Eisner opens with a montage of life in Ogden Marsh set to Johnny Cash's gravelly rendition of Vera Lynn's "We'll Meet

Again"—the song that famously plays over the montage of mushroom clouds at the end of Stanley Kubrick's Cold War satire *Dr. Strangelove, or: How I Learned to Stop Worrying and Love the Bomb* (1964). The implication is that the town is finished before the movie even begins. And indeed, it looks much the same preoutbreak as it does postoutbreak, its empty Main Street and shuttered shops evoking a community whose best days are behind it. Similarly, its contaminated citizens are, until the final stages of their infection, visually indistinguishable from its healthy inhabitants. The town drunk who wanders onto the field with a loaded shotgun during a high school baseball game, the farmer who burns his house down with his wife and young son inside, the trio of redneck hunters who murder indiscriminately and mount their victims like trophies— all look completely normal.

The implication is that the residents' homicidal rage was always there, lurking behind the "Iowa Nice" mask of midwestern civility, a symptom of twenty-first-century socioeconomic malaise just waiting to be unleashed. Once out, it is impossible to contain, as the movie illustrates. In the end, Dutton and his pregnant wife, Judy (Radha Mitchell), manage to escape Ogden Marsh before the military obliterates it with a nuclear device, but a mock satellite feed shows us that Trixie has already spread to their destination, the neighboring city of Cedar Rapids.

Small towns may be the first to fall to late-capitalist rage, *The Crazies* insinuates, but major metropolises aren't far behind.

Indeed, Marc Forster's *World War Z* (2013), the most recent zombie blockbuster—and, with an estimated budget of $190 million, the most expensive to date—demonstrates that the apocalyptic rage sparked by late capitalism has global implications. The film was adapted from Max Brooks's best-selling 2006 novel *World War Z: An Oral History of the Zombie War* but departs from its source in two major ways. Whereas the book is set after the end of a worldwide battle against the living dead and structured as a series of interviews with survivors, the movie takes place in the early days of the outbreak and traces the peregrinations of the former United Nations investigator Gerry Lane (Brad Pitt), who is tasked with combing the globe for clues to the origin and nature of the zombie virus. The other way in which the movie departs from the book is in its reimagining of Brooks's classic "slow" zombies as explosively fast, rabid monsters better described as "consumed" than "consumers." Moving together in swarms, almost as a single organism, they are driven not by the urge to feed on their victims but by the desire to pass their disease on to the uninfected. These changes lend the film a sense of urgency and a focus that are absent in the novel. They also hint at how it has been reshaped as a commentary on the current state of the global economy, one framing late capitalism as a virulent infection that, having spread from the West across much of the world, is in desperate need of a cure.

That apocalyptic capitalism is a central concern in *World War Z* is clear from the start. The film's title sequence juxtaposes images of life in late-capitalist culture (congested freeways, stock-market tickers, celebrity talk shows, civil unrest) with images of violent animal predation (wild dogs fighting over a fresh kill, vultures feasting on carrion, ants cannibalizing a larger insect). It underscores the rapacious nature of capitalism in the twenty-first century, signaling, through its accelerating montage and increasingly ominous score, that such a system is ultimately unsustainable. And in fact the breakdown of late capitalism is precisely what the movie goes on to chronicle. As Gerry travels from the United States to South Korea, Israel, and the United Kingdom in the wake of the outbreak, Forster establishes that while its origin is unknown, the zombie virus is primarily associated with the world's most developed, heavily industrialized, and highly corporatized societies. It's as if capitalism itself is the disease, as if the very behavior that capitalism demands—ruthless competition, unrestrained consumption—has caused the zombie apocalypse rippling across the globe like a cataclysmic market crash. *World War Z* figuratively suggests that capitalism is cannibalizing itself. The film also implies, like the eco-zombie movies discussed earlier, that the virus is perhaps punishment for capitalism's impact on the environment—except in this case, it's not the result of an industrial disaster but rather nature's way of purging a species that has upset its balance.

In any event, it becomes clear that the only remedy is the antithesis of capitalist behavior. As in other recent zombie blockbusters, the key to humanity's survival is a spirit of cooperation and a sense of shared welfare. Gerry must cross borders and forge international alliances to find a cure for the virus, and he stresses in the film's final scenes that the sole hope for victory over the dead lies in collaboration. The film's status as a product of corporate Hollywood notwithstanding, *World War Z* offers a biting critique of late capitalism—one that, if its massive box-office returns (over half a billion dollars worldwide) are any indication, resonated powerfully with global audiences.

There is nothing new about the use of horrific metaphors to capture the monstrousness of capitalism as an economic system. In the first volume of *Capital*, Karl Marx variously describes capitalism as "dripping from head to toe, from every pore, with blood and dirt" (926), as "dead labour which, vampire-like, lives only by sucking living labour" (342), and as nourishing a "werewolf-like hunger" for surplus labor (353). Zombies are just the latest in a long line of capitalist monsters. In many ways, however, they are the most apt. As Steven Shaviro writes, the "life-in-death of the zombie is a nearly perfect allegory for the inner logic of capitalism, whether this be taken in the sense of the exploitation of living labor by dead labor, the deathlike regimentation of factories and other social spaces, or the artificial, externally driven stimulation of consumers" (83).

The cultural logic of late capitalism, in particular, finds ideal embodiment in the cannibalistic zombies introduced by George A. Romero in *Night of the Living Dead* and deployed by legions of filmmakers since. As the ultimate in possessiveness, cannibalism represents, in Robin Wood's words, "the logical end of human relations under capitalism" ("Introduction" 21). All good capitalists are conditioned to live off other people, he notes—zombies "simply carry this to its logical and literal conclusion" (*Hollywood* 289). Like us, the dead "consume *for the sake of consuming*" (Wood, *Hollywood* 289). At the same time, like us, they themselves increasingly seem consumed in the twenty-first century, reflecting the dilemma of an economy nearing its apocalyptic limit. As a commercial product, zombie cinema is inescapably implicated in late capitalism. At its best, however, it provides a space for us to contemplate—and a means for us to address—the way in which the dominant economic order in the West has, zombie-like, lingered on well past its expiration date, feeding on us as we feed, heedlessly, on others.

3

BOY EATS GIRL

The living dead have undergone significant revision in twenty-first-century zombie cinema. These days, they are more likely to sprint than shamble across the screen. They are more often the product of viral infection than voodoo rites or radiation from space. And they are more numerous than ever before, as the zombie apocalypse has gone from local to global in scope. Of all the ways in which the dead have lately been reimagined on film, however, perhaps none is more radical or more fascinating than their transformation into explicitly sexed and gendered monsters. If zombies have typically been depicted as creatures devoid of sex characteristics, they are frequently defined today as biologically male or female. Moreover, they are now routinely assigned gender roles, functioning as husbands, girlfriends, housemaids, manservants, strippers, and schoolgirls.

This is not an incidental development in contemporary zombie cinema. It indicates an unprecedented interest on the part of the genre in relationships between men and women, alive and otherwise. Recent zombie movies, many of them comedies and melodramas rather than straightforward horror films, revolve around lonely housewives who find true love with zombies trained as domestic help, teenage boys who keep zombie girls chained up in the basement as sex slaves, zombie viruses transmitted through sexual intercourse like venereal diseases, and zombie apocalypses pitting women against ravening hordes of living dead men. Even more intriguingly, it points to an unprecedented attention on the part of the genre to the politics of sex and gender. In the new millennium, zombie cinema demonstrates a concern with the status of women in Western culture and beyond that could broadly be described as feminist.

This represents something of a sea change for the zombie film, which has a less-than-stellar record of feminism. In fact, up to the end of the last century, its treatment of sex and gender was generally regressive and reactionary, reflecting a "patriarchal fear of increasing female liberation, suffrage, and the rise of feminism" (Jones, "Porn" 42). Women are reduced by black magic to little more than living dolls at the beck and call of male masters in early zombie movies like Victor Halperin's *White Zombie* (1932) and William Beaudine's *Voodoo Man* (1944). Liberated femininity is framed as the trigger for outbreaks of the living dead in Euro-horror zombie films like Amando de Ossorio's *Tombs of the Blind Dead* (*La noche del terror ciego*, 1972) and Lucio Fulci's *The House by the Cemetery* (*Quella villa accanto al cimitero*, 1981). Latter-day scream queens are offered up as erotic objects for the male gaze in postmodern zombie comedies like Dan O'Bannon's *The Return of the Living Dead* (1985) and Stuart Gordon's *Re-Animator* (1985). And the female body is transformed into a source of horror in cult zombie splatterfests like Sam Raimi's *The Evil Dead* (1981) and Peter Jackson's *Braindead* (1992). There are, of course, movies that conspicuously break with the sexism and misogyny of premillennial zombie cinema, from Jacques Tourneur's *I Walked with a Zombie* (1943), a West Indian version of Charlotte Brontë's *Jane Eyre* with a strong female lead, to Tom Savini's *Night of the Living Dead* (1990), a remake of George A. Romero's 1968 classic that recasts the character of Barbra—who is virtually catatonic in the original—as an action heroine. But these are exceptions; as a rule, the zombie film has traditionally been indifferent or hostile to women.

That is no longer the case. As I show in this chapter, zombie cinema takes a far more progressive approach to issues of sex and gender in the twenty-first century; indeed, it is now frequently critical of male power and privilege, offering sharp observations about the plight of women under patriarchy in the West and elsewhere. In the pages that follow, I consider how recent zombie films, through stories focusing on the lives of the newly sexed and gendered dead, interrogate sexual difference and gender roles, heterosexual romance and marriage, and sexual exploitation and violence in a recognizably feminist fashion. I begin with an analysis of the zom-rom-com, an unlikely combination of the zombie picture and the romantic comedy that has proven quite popular over the past decade or so. Homing in on examples of this hybrid genre that deal with the living falling for the dead and the dead falling for one another, I argue that they metaphorically explore alternatives to romantic norms in patriarchal culture. I then turn my attention to another, less widely recognized offshoot of contemporary zombie cinema that we might call the zombie melodrama or zombie weepie. Examining how this genre draws on established forms of melodrama—especially those associated with the "woman's film"—and crosses them with the zombie movie, I suggest that it is deeply preoccupied with the ways in which women continue to suffer, and to resist, gender-based oppression today. Ultimately, my goal is to show that the zom-rom-com and the zombie weepie each underscore in their own manner the monstrous persistence of the dominant male order in the new millennium, creating a space for us to contemplate patriarchy as a sort of living death.

On the face of it, the romantic comedy and the zombie film seem like a bizarre match. In many respects, however, the pairing makes perfect sense. Comedy and horror are both what Linda Williams has dubbed "body genres"— genres that "sensationally display bodies on the screen and register effects in the bodies of spectators" (4). Their kinship as such is probably most obvious in the correspondence between the gross-out comedy and the gore movie, but it is also evident in resemblance between the romantic comedy and the zombie film: each showcases bodies as objects of desire (be it amorous passion or animal appetite), and each seeks to elicit involuntary bodily responses on the part of the viewer (be it fear and disgust or laughter and tears). Moreover, the romantic comedy and the zombie film, in part because of their focus on the body, have historically shared a low cultural standing. Tamar Jeffers McDonald notes that in the pantheon of popular cinema, romantic comedies have always been among "the lowest of the low" (7), dismissed by critics (particularly male critics) as "chick flicks" or lightweight fluff. Likewise, zombie pictures have long been regarded by the critical establishment as lowbrow fare—mindless entertainment for undiscriminating fans of cinematic trash. Finally, as Rick Altman has shown, the film industry's stock-in-trade is "generating new genres through the monstrous mating of already existing genres," often ones "previously thought diametrically opposed" (5). Why not the romantic comedy and the zombie film? In fact, there is precedent for such a coupling. The zombie comedy dates all the way back to the 1940s, which saw the release of pictures like George Marshall's *The Ghost Breakers* (1940) and Gordon Douglas's *Zombies on Broadway* (1945), and the zombie film was first mixed with romantic comedy in the 1990s in movies like Bob Balaban's *My Boyfriend's Back* (1993) and Michele Soavi's *Cemetery Man* (*Dellamorte dellamore*, 1994). Contemporary producers and directors, no doubt inspired by the massive popularity of both the romantic comedy and the zombie film in recent years, have simply formalized the union, cementing the zom-rom-com's status as a hybrid genre.

What I find fascinating is that the marriage of these two genres opens up avenues of female agency and liberation seemingly foreclosed in each individually. As already discussed, the zombie film has not characteristically been progressive in its treatment of women. The romantic comedy, in contrast, has been—one thinks, for instance, of the strong female protagonists at the center of classic screwball comedies like Howard Hawks's *Bringing Up Baby* (1938) or New Hollywood comedies like Woody Allen's *Annie Hall* (1977). But since the late 1980s, it has taken what McDonald describes as a "neo-traditionalist" turn, cultivating a veneer of modern sophistication while nostalgically reviving the "standard myths about romance" (87). As Steve Neale points out, the dominant ideological tendency of the genre now lies "in countering any 'threat' of female independence, and in securing most of its female characters for traditional female roles" (298). Although there are certainly recent romantic comedies that work to subvert the genre's "passionate conformism" (Krutnik 144), the bulk of them lend impetus to the contemporary postfeminist "reinforcement of conservative norms as the ultimate 'best choices' in women's lives" (Negra 4). Intriguingly, this is frequently not the case with zom-rom-coms, which in exploring the love lives of the living and the dead demonstrate that there are other options open to women. If the standard "boy meets girl" formula of the neo-traditional romantic comedy tends to serve patriarchal interests in spite of its superficial commitment to female independence, the "boy eats girl" formula of the zom-rom-com—surprisingly—makes room for a brand of feminism completely at odds with the zombie film's history of sexism and misogyny. Indeed, in the zom-rom-com, the living dead are often a girl's best friend.

This is not to say that zom-rom-coms are uniformly progressive in their treatment of sex and gender. Actually, some of the best known examples of the genre are marked by the same kind of ideological conservatism associated with the neo-traditional romantic comedy. For example, Edgar Wright's cult favorite *Shaun of the Dead* (2004), arguably the film most responsible for launching the zom-rom-com as a popular cinematic hybrid in the twenty-first century, is rather retrograde from a feminist perspective. Its concern is ultimately in reuniting the title character, an unambitious slacker, with his ex-girlfriend, who dumps him at the beginning of the movie because he spends more time at the local pub with his best mate than he does with her. A zombie outbreak provides him with the opportunity to "take charge" and win her back, which he does without changing his ways in the least; in the end, she simply accepts (and adopts) his lackadaisical attitude. A similar dynamic animates Ruben Fleischer's hit zom-rom-com *Zombieland* (2009), whose geeky male protagonist overcomes his phobias (both where the living dead and the opposite sex are concerned) to find true love in the middle of a zombie apocalypse; he is able to woo the feisty, fiercely independent woman of his dreams by rescuing her from the clutches of the dead at the movie's climax. And it also informs Burr Steers's recent, action-driven zom-rom-com *Pride and Prejudice and Zombies* (2016), which, like its literary source—the Seth Grahame-Smith novel of the same title—features a postfeminist heroine who is "physically strong, capable of independence, and yet still chained to the necessity of finding the ideal mate" (Ruthven 341).

As high profile as these films are, however, they are not representative of the zom-rom-com as a genre. In fact, all three fall into a single category of zom-rom-coms that Christian Lenz has labeled the "human-human" zom-rom-com, a variant in which two humans fall in love during a time of zombie crisis, brought together by their shared struggle against living dead—who "present an important plot point device, yet . . . are not the focus: they are the means but nothing else" (108). This brand of zom-rom-com, Lenz writes, traffics in "boy meets girl" stories very close to those found in the neo-traditional romantic comedy and "still enforces gender stereotypes: the male is the active part and the female is to be rescued" (108). Conversely, other categories of zom-rom-com— those devoted to what Lenz calls "human-zombie" and "zombie-zombie" romance—largely break from such patriarchal paradigms. They open up "a new direction for the otherwise retrograde romantic comedy" by using "the zombie as the Other to show that there are other forms of companionship and relationship" (Lenz 115). Although the films that fall into these categories are perhaps less familiar to viewers, I argue that they better capture the zom-rom-com's feminist potential as a genre.

That potential is already evident in David Gebroe's *Zombie Honeymoon* (2004), a low-budget indie zom-rom-com released (to much less fanfare) the same year as

Shaun of the Dead. It offers a campy, tragicomic take on heterosexual marriage as a patriarchal institution. The film concerns a pair of hip young newlyweds, Denise (Tracy Coogan) and Danny (Graham Sibley), who head to the Jersey Shore for their honeymoon after getting hitched. Their postnuptial bliss is short-lived. On their first day at the beach, Danny is attacked by a zombie that emerges from the surf and vomits a black bile into his mouth as he is sunbathing, killing him; miraculously, he comes back to life, but Denise's relief turns to horror when he develops an uncontrollable craving for human flesh and slowly begins to rot away.

Zombie Honeymoon can be read as a movie about how man and wife alike are made monstrous by marriage. An exuberant couple deliriously in love at the outset of the film, Denise and Danny discover that matrimony is hell. Danny literally becomes a monster once they're married, devolving into a flesh-eating ghoul who's finally as dangerous to Denise as he is to their friends and neighbors. Meanwhile, Denise develops into a monstrous enabler of her husband's cannibalistic behavior, staying with him and covering up his crimes. Their hopes and dreams, including a long-planned move to Portugal, fade as both are essentially zombified by wedlock. It's not difficult to see the film as a commentary on marriage as a kind of living death, one that—in part because of how it fosters monstrous masculinity—saps romance, converting living relationships into dead ones.

At the same time, one could also argue that the zombie serves as an instrument of female liberation in *Zombie Honeymoon*. Danny's zombification loosens the patriarchal constraints of traditional marriage, allowing for Denise's eventual emancipation. Tellingly, it appears to be precipitated by a fanciful sketch that Denise does of Danny on his surfboard, menaced by a large, black bird of prey. It's just as she is finishing the drawing that the zombie materializes from the water, suggesting that she has somehow willed it into existence—and that its attack on Danny represents a sort of wish fulfillment on her part. Her short red wedding dress, her profession as a comic-book illustrator, and her love of punk music all mark her as a free spirit and an unconventional woman; it seems quite possible that despite her obvious love for Danny, she unconsciously feels trapped by their marriage. It's clear by the end of the movie, at any rate, that she is determined to live on her own terms. Rather than succumbing to grief after Danny's zombieism finally claims his life, she opts to fulfill their longtime dream by traveling to Portugal alone. The cover of Tammy Wynette's "Stand by Your Man" that plays over the closing credits as Denise makes her way to the airport underscores, ironically, how far past such patriarchal sentiment she is.

Thanks to the zombie she conjures up, she only has to endure the bonds of marriage to Danny until living death does them part.

The zombie is also an agent of female liberation in Andrew Currie's *Fido* (2006), a Canadian zom-rom-com that brilliantly satirizes traditional marriage as a means of patriarchal containment. Set in an alternate universe where a zombie apocalypse occurred in the 1950s, it imagines an Eisenhower-era America in which small towns are fenced off from the dead-infested "wild zone" outside, schoolchildren are taught how to aim for the head in case of a zombie attack, families save up for funeral services (including decapitation and separate "head coffins") that ensure they won't come back after death, and zombies tamed with "domestication collars" work as servants, milkmen, newspaper boys, and factory laborers. Social order is maintained by a giant corporation called Zomcon, which promises "a better life through containment."

But when we're introduced to one of this world's settlements, the bustling burg of Willard, it quickly becomes clear that containment is not all it's cracked up to be. Outwardly an idyllic suburban utopia, the community is actually a hotbed of hypocrisy, intolerance, envy, and resentment whose inhabitants lead lives of quiet desperation. In the case of the Robinson family, picture-perfect appearances mask a particularly deep unhappiness: little

Timmy (K'Sun Ray) is bullied at school; his emotionally distant father, Bill (Dylan Baker), obsesses over funeral payments; and his insecure mother, Helen (Carrie-Anne Moss), continually frets about their social standing. Everything changes, however, after Helen splurges on the family's first zombie. Purchased as a status symbol and a home convenience, Fido (Billy Connolly) ultimately offers a cure for the repression and conformism that define the family's existence.

Most in need of such a cure is Helen, who plainly feels trapped in her role as the model mother and housewife. Taking a cue from Douglas Sirk's *All That Heaven Allows* (1955), a classic melodrama about a well-to-do widow who falls in love with her working-class gardener, *Fido* focuses on how Helen finds freedom and happiness through a taboo-breaking relationship with her zombie. At first, conditioned by society's contempt for the dead, she simply regards him as "the help." Over time, though, she comes to prefer him to her husband, a zombie-phobe who spends all his time on the golf course when he's not sweating the details of his funeral. Fido turns out to be a better father than Bill—a true friend and protector to Timmy. He also turns out to be a better romantic partner for her. Their chemistry is evident when Helen dresses him in one of Bill's suits for a drive in the country and when they dance to swing music in her living room.

As viewers, we root for them to end up together. No doubt Billy Connolly's charming performance, which recalls Charlie Chaplin's as the Little Tramp or Boris Karloff's as the Frankenstein monster in its reliance on silent pantomime, is one reason. As unlikely as it sounds, he makes it easy to see Fido as Mr. Right. But it's mostly because we understand that the couple's love represents a rejection of "the corset of values of [the] time [and] the fake morality [of a] facade-obsessed society" (Lenz 110). Helen's relationship with Fido is not about sexual attraction, chiefly, but about mutual respect and a shared affirmation that they each possess value beyond their socially prescribed roles. We want them to live happily ever after because they deserve to in a world where women and the dead alike are treated as second-class citizens. And because this is a romantic comedy, we get what we want: when Bill meets with an untimely demise and receives the funeral he's always wanted, Helen and Fido have their fairy-tale ending. In fact, their happiness proves contagious, inspiring others in the neighborhood to "go zombie" as well. *Fido* finally frames romance not just as personal liberation but as a platform for social change.

The feminist potential of the "human-zombie" zom-rom-com is obvious. It has the capacity to reconfigure heterosexual romance and marriage, opening up alternatives to traditional gender roles for women. To a certain extent, however, the prospects of the female characters in these films remain limited by the imperatives of patriarchal culture. Denise is free of her conjugal bonds at the end of *Zombie Honeymoon*, but all she can imagine doing is traveling to Portugal as she and Danny originally planned; her horizons continue to be circumscribed by her life with her husband. Similarly, although Helen has found a more congenial male partner by the end of *Fido*, she is still defined primarily as a wife and mother in the film's final scene. The boundaries placed on female liberation are even more pronounced in other "human-zombie" zom-rom-coms. For example, in Jonathan Levine's Romeo-and-Juliet tale *Warm Bodies* (2013), the radical implications of the heroine's "star-crossed" romance with her zombie lover are negated when his passion for her turns him back into an ordinary man, while in Joe Dante's overtly misogynistic *Burying the Ex* (2014), the zombie is a "crazy ex-girlfriend" who must be done away with so the male hero can be with the woman he really loves.

A more revolutionary brand of feminism can be found in the last category of zom-rom-com identified by Lenz: the "zombie-zombie" romantic comedy. Here, the focus is on love among the living dead in a "community outside the human realm where they can be themselves according to their own rules without the interference of humans" (114). This brand of zom-rom-com doesn't so much transform as transcend the conventions of heterosexual romance and marriage. It locates a space for male-female relationships outside of patriarchal culture.

Take the example of Elza Kephart's *Graveyard Alive* (2003), one of the few zombie movies to date directed by a woman. Gorgeously shot in black-and-white Techniscope, the film is an affectionate send-up of television soap operas like *General Hospital* (1963–), complete with hammy performances, canned dialogue—and zombies. It tells the story of Patsy Powers (Anne Day-Jones), a shy, frumpy nurse who harbors a secret crush on the hunky Dr. Dox (Karl Gerhardt), her hospital's star physician; he took her to the prom in high school but now only has eyes for the pretty, popular nurse Goodie Tueschuze (Samantha Slan), his fiancée and the daughter of the hospital's head administrator. Patsy's chance to get her man back comes when she is bitten by a zombified logger who is admitted to the emergency room with an axe in his head. Along with an insatiable hunger for human flesh, she develops a seductive new look that soon gets Dr. Dox's attention; unfortunately, she needs to feed on fresh meat to maintain her sex appeal, and the jealous Goodie quickly grows suspicious about her secretive visits to the morgue.

At first, *Graveyard Alive* seems very much like a traditional love story, with two women vying for the same man in a battle that's all about which can be the more physically attractive. But it turns out to be something more subversive than that. The zombie makeover that transforms Patsy into a sexy femme fatale and has all of the men at the hospital panting after her—literally, in one funny scene—also rewires her thinking about romance. As a zombie bombshell, she has no particular use for men, sexually; she desires only to bite them, to convert them into the living dead as well. This is the case with the male orderly she gives a good-night nip after an evening of karaoke. It's even the case with Dr. Dox, when she finally lands a date with the man of her dreams. Invited over to his house for dinner, she finds herself frankly disgusted by his dirty laundry and sloppy eating habits, as well as his smarmy attempts at seduction. Her fantasies about him now involve her sinking her teeth into his torso in the bathtub. And after she does finally zombify him, she ceremonially burns the photo of the two of them at prom that she's kept in her locker, signifying that she's moved beyond a romantic dependency on men—that such a notion no longer has a place, or even meaning, in her new life as a dead woman.

But Patsy's zombification leads to more than just her own feminist awakening. At the end of the movie, when Goodie returns to the hospital after a stint in the loony bin (where she was placed by her father after accusing Patsy of being a zombie), she discovers that it has been converted from a place of male power and privilege to an egalitarian community of the dead unbound by conventional definitions of sex and gender. As Goodie is inducted into their ranks in the final scene, the film fades to black—perhaps suggesting that this community is ultimately unrepresentable as a utopian space. The impression we're left with, though, is that this has been a story not only about personal empowerment but also about social revolution.

The same impression is evoked by Matthew Kohnen's supremely silly *Aaah! Zombies!!* (2007). It concerns four best friends who accidentally ingest a top-secret serum that was designed by the military to create supersoldiers but that has the unfortunate side effect of turning anyone exposed to it into a flesh-eating ghoul. Much of the humor of the film derives from the fact that its heroes—the awkward neurotic Tim (Michael Grant Terry), the cynical slacker Mike (Matthew Davis), the aspiring professional Vanessa (Julianna Robinson), and the bubbly animal lover Cindy (Betsy Beutler)—fail to realize for most of the movie that they are dead. Instead, noticing that everyone around them now seems to move and speak unnaturally rapidly, they believe that the rest of Los Angeles has been infected by some sort of viral plague. Kohnen underlines the comic irony by presenting their point of view (in which the four appear completely normal) in color and the point of view of the humans they meet (in which the four appear as shuffling, moaning zombies) in black and white. Interestingly, when they finally discover the truth, rather than going in search of a cure for their condition, they embrace it, erecting a town in the desert where they and others who have been transformed by the serum can exist in peace. And the viewer cheers them on. By the end of the movie, we've come not only to identify with its zombified protagonists but also to regard the bright, colorful world of the dead as preferable in every way to the drab, monochrome world of the living.

What makes *Aaah! Zombies!!* intriguing in spite of its broad and often sophomoric comedy is the way in which it uses the notion of zombieism as the next step in human evolution to explore the possibility of a romantic relationship between men and women beyond the bounds of patriarchal tradition. That the film regards living death as a new stage in human development is clear from an animated opening sequence that imagines an evolutionary chain beginning with a chimpanzee, who is followed by a hominid, who is followed by a caveman, who is followed by a modern man on a cellphone, who is followed by a zombie (who promptly eats his predecessor's brain). And it just as quickly establishes its interest in finding a romantic solution for its four protagonists, who at the start form a pair of failed couples. Although Tim has loved Cindy for the past ten years, he's been unable to tell her so; meanwhile, Mike and Vanessa broke up a year earlier but are still in love. It's clear that these couples belong together, yet it's not until they become zombies that true romance is possible. Living death, it seems, is the key to love.

Crucially, however, it's not the type of love they would have shared as humans, in that it's wholly free of the patriarchal imperatives of male pleasure and female procreation. As rotting zombies, Tim loses his penis and Mike is finally reduced to a bodiless head, but it makes no difference in their new relationships—Cindy shrugs off the loss of Tim's manhood while Vanessa simply carries Mike's head around in a bowling-ball bag outfitted with eyeholes. Cindy and Vanessa, for their part, presumably can no longer bear children and are thus unable to fulfill their socially mandated role as mothers; this, though, does not seem to bother Tim and Mike in the least. As Lenz puts it, theirs is now "a love rooted solely in the person" (113). Significantly, this enlightened brand of romance is linked in the film to radical social transformation. At the end of the movie, the zombie lovers rally their fellow dead around the "chance to start anew," to build a "zombie society where everyone is equal, separate from the intolerance and hatred of the outside world." Like *Graveyard Alive*, *Aaah! Zombies!!* closes in utopian fashion, with a vision of a living-dead community that is feminist in its egalitarianism. As a zom-rom-com, it once again demonstrates the capacity of the genre not just to transform but to transcend the dominant patriarchal order.

The zombie romantic comedy is not the only type of twenty-first-century zombie cinema to challenge traditional configurations of sex and gender, though. A similar feminist bent is evident in another, emerging genre hybrid, the zombie melodrama—or zombie weepie. The zombie weepie mates the zombie movie with the "woman's film," a mode of melodrama that, as Maria LaPlace writes, is "distinguished by its female protagonist, female point of view and its narrative which most often revolves around the traditional realism of women's experience: the familial, the domestic, the romantic—those arenas where love, emotion and relationships take precedence over action and events" (139). The woman's film might seem like a strange match for the zombie movie, but as with the zombie movie and the romantic comedy, the two have more in common than meets the eye. Like the zombie movie, the woman's film is a body genre, marked "by 'excesses' of spectacle and displays of primal, even infantile emotions, and by narratives that seem circular and repetitive" (L. Williams 3). Like the zombie movie, the woman's film has historically had a low cultural standing, reflecting critics' (especially male critics') "lack of respect for women—their experience, work, and art" (Walsh 35).

And like the zombie movie, the woman's film has long enjoyed a mass appeal, making a pairing of the two logical from a commercial standpoint. While zombie weepies have not yet achieved the broad popularity of zom-rom-coms, they have grown steadily in number over the past decade or so, signaling that mainstream success may be right around the corner.

As with the zom-rom-com, what I find interesting about the zombie weepie is that it treats issues of sex and gender more progressively than either the zombie movie or the woman's film do. One might expect an impressive record of feminism from the woman's film, especially in comparison with the zombie movie. Despite the genre's focus on women's lives and issues, however, it often frames femininity as something to be contained and recuperated by patriarchal institutions. Frequently revolving, as Linda Williams notes, around the "case of the woman 'afflicted' with a deadly or debilitating disease," it connects female agency with "bodily hysteria or excess," presenting it as an illness in need of a cure (4). The zombie weepie, too, routinely pathologizes women (as the living dead); moreover, unlike the zom-rom-com, it typically doesn't allow them happy endings, trading romantic rapture for grim pathos. Where it departs from the woman's film (and the zombie movie) is in its use of female misfortune and monstrosity to critique male hegemony. The zombie weepie may feature women as the dead, but it makes clear that the real monsters are men. The remainder of this chapter surveys four ways in which the zombie movie has recently combined with the woman's film to depict patriarchy as a kind of living death.

The first type of contemporary zombie weepie that bears mention mates the zombie movie with one of the most controversial forms of the woman's film: the rape-revenge picture. A genre in which "a rape that is central to the narrative is punished by an act of vengeance, either by the victim themselves or by an agent (a lawyer, policeman, or, most commonly, a loved one or family member" (Heller-Nicholas 3), rape-revenge is generally associated with horror, particularly seventies exploitation movies like Wes Craven's *The Last House on the Left* (1972) and Meir Zarchi's *I Spit on Your Grave* (1978). But as Alexandra Heller-Nicholas has shown, it began as a branch of the woman's film, coalescing in pre-Code weepies like William A. Wellman's *Safe in Hell* (1931) and Stephen Roberts's *The Story of Temple Drake* (1933) and postwar melodramas like Jean Negulesco's *Johnny Belinda* (1948) and Ida Lupino's *Outrage* (1950) (13–19).

Although rape-revenge movies (especially the more exploitative ones) have often been denounced as tasteless and misogynistic, critics like Carol J. Clover find in them surprising signs of feminism, pointing out that they "not only have female heroes and male villains [but also] repeatedly and explicitly articulate feminist politics" (151). Such politics are particularly prominent in the twenty-first-century zombie rape-revenge film. Mindless and lifeless, the female zombie may seem like an unlikely agent of feminist change. Both as suffering victim and as monstrous avenger, however, she embodies a powerful critique of the patriarchal exploitation and oppression of women.

This critique becomes abundantly clear in the most notorious zombie rape-revenge movie of the new millennium to date, Marcel Sarmiento and Gadi Harel's *Deadgirl* (2008). The film concerns two teenage friends, Rickie (Shiloh Fernandez) and JT (Noah Segan), who discover a naked female zombie (Jenny Spain), gagged and wrapped in plastic in the basement of an abandoned mental hospital. Horrified, Rickie wants to call the police, but a fascinated JT insists, "We could keep her." Dubbing the zombie "Deadgirl," JT chains her to a bed in the basement, where he rapes her repeatedly; eventually, he brings in another friend, Wheeler (Eric Podnar), who also uses her as a "fuck slave." The conflicted Rickie refuses to join in but can't help fantasizing about his longtime crush Joann (Candice Accola)—who's dating the popular jock Johnny (Andrew DiPalma)—as his own private sex zombie. Perversely, he gets his wish when JT and Wheeler realize that a bite from their Deadgirl will make another and kidnap Joann as their next victim. *Deadgirl* is stomach churning in its portrayal of sexual violation and appears on the surface to confirm critics' condemnation of rape-revenge as a "licensed form of violence in which a woman acts out male desires for the erotic satisfaction of a predominantly male mass audience" (Lehman 114). Indeed, the very idea of a female zombie sex slave seems to play into—even to sanction—male fantasies involving the sexual objectification and domination of women.

But in more than one way, the film works against such fantasies, advancing a recognizably feminist agenda. In the first place, Deadgirl is anything but a passive, pliant victim. She displays, in Jenny Spain's astonishing performance, a feral rage in captivity, as well as a baleful hatred for her rapists. JT and Wheeler find her steady, returned gaze—that she looks at them "like she knows something"—unnerving and her physical resistance daunting. She never ceases to struggle against them, growling, snapping, and scratching even as they beat her. And like the female victims in other rape-revenge films, she eventually turns the tables on her tormentors. She castrates Johnny when he forces her to perform oral sex on him during a visit to the basement, and after she gets free of her bonds at the end of the film, she cannibalizes both JT and Wheeler, violating their bodies with her zombie virus. "I can feel her inside me," a dying JT whimpers when Rickie finds him.

In addition, as Steve Jones notes, despite Deadgirl's monstrousness, masculinity is "the film's primary site of horror" ("Gender" 534). Every major male character in the movie engages in or fantasizes about rape, hinting that sexual violence is not a question of a few "bad apples" but a cultural norm. Tellingly, JT describes the opportunity for "hot pussy" that Deadgirl offers as like something "straight out of porn." Not even Rickie, the most sympathetic male character in the film, is immune to the influence of a culture that promotes the exploitation and oppression of women: rather than saving Joann at the end of the picture, he has the infected JT bite her, making her his personal Deadgirl. Ultimately, the movie shows that manhood continues to be defined in the West and elsewhere by a social "pressure to assert sexual dominance over women" (Jones, "Gender" 533), proving that even a controversial zombie rape-revenge film can serve feminist ends.

The zombie maternal melodrama, a second type of zombie weepie to appear in recent years, also possesses a strong feminist dimension. It blends the zombie movie with the maternal melodrama, a popular subgenre of the woman's film that again dates back to the Hollywood studio era, with roots in such pictures as King Vidor's *Stella*

Dallas (1937) and Michael Curtiz's *Mildred Pierce* (1945). As defined by Mary Ann Doane, maternal melodramas are "scenarios of separation, of separation and return, or of threatened separation—dramas which play out all the permutations of the mother/child relation" (73). Because these films revolve so relentlessly around maternal sacrifice and self-effacement, with mothers giving up everything for the sake of their husbands and children, they have sometimes been read as antifeminist, as paeans to the patriarchal cult of motherhood.

But Doane and others have shown that in the maternal melodrama, motherhood, "far from being the simple locus of comfort and nostalgic pleasure—a position to which a patriarchal culture ceaselessly and somewhat desperately attempts to confine it—is a site of multiple contradictions" (81–82). The zombie maternal melodrama further complicates normative notions about motherhood by replacing the traditional mother with the zombie mom. A figure who—to borrow a famous line from *Stella Dallas*—is quite literally "something else besides a mother," the zombie mom both exposes the monstrousness of maternity under patriarchal rule and makes it possible to imagine a motherhood beyond the dominant male order.

Consider the case of *Miss Zombie* (2013), a fascinating zombie maternal melodrama directed by the Japanese filmmaker Sabu. Shot for the most part in stark mono-chrome, it envisions—like *Fido* but in a far-darker register—a world in which the living dead have been tamed as domestic help. The film opens with a docile female zombie (Ayaka Komatsu) being delivered to the modern, upscale home of the distinguished physician Dr. Teramoto (Toru Tezuka). Teramoto's wife, Shizuko (Makoto Togashi), immediately puts her to work scrub-bing the flagstones on the outdoor patio. She is also expected to entertain the couple's young son, Kenichi (Riku Onishi). At the end of each day, Shizuko gives her a grocery bag full of rotten vegetables to eat, and she trudges to her small, dingy apartment in a nearby town; on the way, local schoolchildren pelt her with rocks, and teenage thugs stick her with pens, screwdrivers, and knives, which she methodically removes at home.

Before long, Teramoto's hired men, aroused by the sight of the zombie bent over the flagstones at work, rape her in the garden shed. Witnessing this, Teramoto himself begins to violate her in the privacy of his study. A photograph in her possession reveals that she was happily married and pregnant in life; we learn from a series of flashbacks, however, that she lost her husband and unborn child to the same mob of feral zombies that "turned" her. In death, she has become a grotesque par-ody of a wife and mother, expected to work tirelessly in the home and sexually service her male master without complaint. The film frames the zombie mom—silent, submissive, and long-suffering—as the maternal "ideal" under patriarchy, underscoring how monstrous its conception of motherhood is.

At the same time, *Miss Zombie* makes clear that the zombie mom's "model" motherhood conceals a sharp feminist edge. Her presence in Teramoto's home soon disrupts the domestic status quo. Initially, it's a question of her sheer passivity and unquestioning obedience. Her slow, painstaking work on the patio, captured in long takes over a series of repetitive scenes, quickly grows oppressive. Even when she's not visible to the family inside, the incessant sound of her scrubbing fills the house; meanwhile, her silence—her refusal to engage with them—becomes its own kind of provocation. Then she begins to displace Shizuko as wife and mother. Having found the "perfect" woman, Teramoto shows little interest in his real spouse. And when Kenichi accidentally drowns one day while at play and is revived by a bite from the zombie, he transfers his affection to her, sitting with her as she works and snapping pictures of them together with his Polaroid camera. Shizuko, robbed of the roles that defined her place in the home, spends her days in a stupor on the couch.

Conversely, the zombie stirs to life, galvanized by her maternal relationship with the undead Kenichi, who triggers memories of the child she lost. To procure the blood he now needs to survive, she kills her teenage tormentors, stalking them at night with the knives they stuck in her. And when a jealous Shizuko shoots Tera-moto and comes after her with the gun, she flees with the boy. In the end, Shizuko, realizing that her son pre-fers his zombie mom, stops the pursuit by shooting her-self. But in the movie's only color sequence, the zombie bites her, reuniting her with her son in living death. It's the sort of sacrificial gesture closely associated with the maternal melodrama; here, though, it's inflected by the zombie film. Rather than serving to reinforce the patri-archal order, it enables a motherhood beyond patriarchy, making the monstrousness of the zombie mom a potent catalyst for feminist change.

A similar kind of revisionism is evident in a third emerging type of zombie weepie, this one drawing on the fallen-woman film. Lea Jacobs describes the fallen-woman picture as an offshoot of the woman's film, typically concerning a female protagonist "who commits a sexual transgression such as adultery or premarital sex. In traditional versions of the plot, she is expelled from the domestic space of the family and undergoes a protracted decline. Alone on the streets, she becomes an outcast, often a prostitute, suffering various humiliations which usually culminate in her death" (x). The product of a long tradition in literature and onstage, the fallen-woman film emerged as a genre of popular cinema during the pre-Code era, with "kept woman" stories and "sex" pictures like Robert Z. Leonard's *Susan Lenox (Her Fall and Rise)* (1931) and John M. Stahl's *Back Street* (1932).

Such "crime-and-punishment cryfests" (Doherty 130) allowed for the representation of "female aggressivity, ambition, and illicit sexuality" (Jacobs 149) but more often than not upheld the patriarchal ideal of female purity by ensuring that the "erring woman was irredeemably punished" (Jacobs 5). The zombie fallen-woman film, on the other hand, may end tragically for its female protagonist but makes plain that patriarchy is to blame for her fate. Usually focusing on a heroine who contracts a zombie virus because of a sexual encounter with an infected man, it presents the fallen woman as a symptom of a male-dominated society that continues to sanction the exploitation and degradation of women.

David Robert Mitchell's *It Follows* (2014) offers an unconventional yet trenchant example of the zombie fallen-woman film. Reminiscent of the early work of David Cronenberg, whose *Shivers* (1975) and *Rabid* (1977) recast zombieism as a sexual disease—its unsettling widescreen compositions and vertiginous camerawork visually evoke John Carpenter and Brian De Palma films of the same vintage—the movie centers on Jay

(Maika Monroe), a teenage girl living in the Detroit suburbs who becomes the victim of a curse when she sleeps
with her new boyfriend, Hugh (Jake Weary). After she
has sex with him, she is followed by a zombie-like creature that is only visible to her and can look like anyone;
Hugh tells her that it will kill her if it catches her and that
her only hope is to pass on the curse by having sex with
someone else. If she dies, the curse will revert back to him.
Desperate to stop the monster's slow, inexorable progress
toward her but reluctant to spread the curse further, Jay
turns to her sister Kelly (Lili Sepe) and friends Paul (Keir
Gilchrist), Yara (Olivia Luccardi), and Greg (Daniel
Zovatto) for help in figuring out how to get rid of it.

It Follows has been interpreted allegorically as a post-
AIDS cautionary tale about the dangers of sexually
transmitted disease. I suggest that it also reworks the
fallen-woman film for the twenty-first century, evoking
the way in which female sexuality, although superficially
"liberated," is still very much subject to punishment in
contemporary American culture. While Mitchell establishes that men and women alike are susceptible to the
zombie curse, the film focuses in far more detail on its
female victims. Foremost among them is Jay, who, following sex with Hugh, is the monster's target for most of the
movie. But she is not the only one. The picture opens with
the zombie claiming another female teenager, whom we

later discover is Hugh's previous girlfriend. The creature also seems at certain points to take on the form of other women it has killed. In a memorable scene, it appears in Jay's kitchen as a woman whose face is bloodied and bruised, whose hands are bound behind her back, and whose clothing is ripped, leaving one breast exposed. Like the traditional fallen-woman film, *It Follows* demonstrates that for women, sex is inevitably followed by suffering. Jay's harrowing ordeal—the zombie's relentless pursuit ultimately forces her to sleep with a series of men in an effort to shake the curse—in particular drives home how little attitudes toward female sexuality have changed since the last century.

Unlike the traditional fallen-woman film, however, Mitchell's movie is distinctly critical of those attitudes. To begin with, we are clearly meant to identify with Jay's struggle against her zombie curse. Maika Monroe's sympathetic performance in the lead role and the frequent point-of-view shots that align us with her character's perspective ensure that we never feel she "deserves" the suffering she endures. Moreover, the film places the blame for Jay's suffering squarely on patriarchal culture. Primarily responsible is Hugh, who passed the curse not only to her but also to his previous girlfriend. But the zombie itself also frequently functions as the avatar of an oppressive male order, at one point taking on the shape of a neighborhood boy who spies on Jay as she swims in her backyard pool and dresses in her bathroom and at another appearing as her absent father. In the latter incarnation, it literally embodies punitive patriarchal authority, hurling household objects at her—irons, lamps, televisions—as she and her friends attempt to trap and kill it. Even Paul and Greg, who arguably take advantage of Jay's predicament to sleep with her, exhibit signs of monstrous masculinity. Indeed, near the end of the film, Paul essentially becomes a new Hugh when, having intentionally contracted the zombie virus through consensual sex with Jay, he attempts to pass it on to an unsuspecting female prostitute.

As in *Deadgirl*, the monstrous-masculine is linked to porn, which Jay and Paul talk about encountering as children in one scene and which Jay and her friends discover at an abandoned house used as a refuge by Hugh in another. And, significantly, it's rooted in the suburbs. Whereas the danger zone in the classic fallen-woman film is the city, Detroit is a dilapidated, depopulated ruin in this movie. The real threat is to be found where "father knows best": behind white picket fences and manicured lawns. Supposedly safe for women, suburbia is anything but, as the final shot of the picture emphasizes. Jay and Paul, believing themselves to be free of the curse at last, are walking hand in hand on their street when a figure appears in the background, following them—an apt metaphor for the surveillance and discipline that women still face under patriarchy today.

The critique of patriarchy undertaken in the types of zombie melodrama discussed so far is perhaps most explicit in a fourth and final variety: the zombie paranoid woman's film. A product of the postwar era, the paranoid woman's film channeled women's fears that the social and economic gains they had seen during World War II would be erased when their husbands, fathers, sons, and brothers returned home. Featuring "victimized, mad, or terrified women, and usually set in ornate, claustrophobic interiors," classic examples of the genre, such as Robert Siodmak's *The Spiral Staircase* (1945) and Fritz Lang's *Secret beyond the Door* (1947), express a "distrust in love and family relationships" and posit that the true threat to their female protagonists "is close to home and usually male" (Walsh 170).

The paranoid woman's film has been of interest to feminist scholars because it focuses on women who struggle against patriarchal villains. At the same time, there is widespread recognition that, as Doane writes, the "woman's exercise of an active investigating gaze can only be simultaneous with her own victimisation" (136). In fact, the heroine is typically victimized twice in these movies: first by the villainous man she battles and then by the patriarchal society that reclaims her in the end. The zombie paranoid woman's film both amplifies and transforms the genre. Envisaging the zombie apocalypse as an epic battle of the sexes, in which female protagonists must fend off ravening hordes of living-dead men, it too examines the plight of women in a hostile "man's world." Rather than insisting on the subjugation and recuperation of its heroines, though, it depicts them transcending male oppression and working, often in concert, to dismantle the dominant patriarchal order.

The Japanese zombie paranoid woman's film *Schoolgirl Apocalypse* (*Sêrâ-fuku mokushiroku*, 2011), directed by the American expatriate filmmaker John Cairns, represents a case in point. It tells the story of Sakura (Higarino), a teenage girl living in a mountain village who is forced to fend for herself when a strange signal emanating from the sea turns every man in Japan into a murderous zombie. Armed with the bow she uses for archery practice at school, she manages not only to survive but also to uncover the source of the zombie signal, which is linked to a mysterious boy named Billy (Max Mackenzie) who haunts her animated dreams. Like a classic paranoid woman's film, *Schoolgirl Apocalypse* quickly establishes that its heroine faces a male threat close to home—only here the men are *literally* monsters.

Sakura is first attacked by her zombified father, who, when he returns home from work at the beginning of the movie, immediately stabs her mother to death and attempts to strangle her. After escaping her house, she finds that her small town is no safer. She stumbles across her best friend, who has been battered by her little brother. She meets a woman who has bound and gagged her young son because he mauled her leg. Formerly trusted male figures—policemen, teachers, postal workers, schoolboys—now target her, and other women, with homicidal rage. It is as though the misogyny lurking just under the surface of patriarchal culture has been personified and given free rein. Significantly, we are asked not simply to bear witness to this violence against women but to experience it firsthand. Using point-of-view shots, Cairns has us share Sakura's perspective, for example, when she is choked by her father. As his face looms over us in close-up, contorted in hate, it feels as if we too are being assaulted. The movie makes female victimization, a staple of the paranoid woman's film, terrifyingly real for viewers.

Unlike the paranoid woman's film, however, *Schoolgirl Apocalypse* does not compound its female protagonist's victimization by insisting in the end on her reabsorption by the dominant male order. Instead, the zombie apocalypse acts as a rite of passage that helps Sakura develop into a strong, independent young woman—one who takes on patriarchy and wins. The figure of the uniformed

Japanese schoolgirl, routinely fetishized in film and pop culture as an erotic object, emerges here as an empowered subject. A shy, timid teenager when the outbreak occurs, Sakura learns to defend herself against the male zombies prowling the countryside. Relying on her dreams for guidance, she locates the real Billy and in a neat gender reversal rescues him from the crazed, katana-wielding bad girl Aoi (Mai Tsujimoto). And when she discovers in the film's surreal finale that Billy is not a boy at all but a sea monster in human form—a tentacled, leech-like creature who has been feeding on his female caretakers and whose keening mother is the source of the zombie signal—she dispatches him with an arrow and throws his body into the ocean, terminating the signal and ending his influence over her and Aoi. The final shot of the movie, which shows Sakura striding confidently along the beach, bow in hand, attests that while the zombie weepie is in many ways the flip side of the zom-rom-com, it also has the capacity to imagine happy endings for its heroines.

The explicit sexing and gendering of the living dead in twenty-first-century zombie cinema is a development that has been largely overlooked in feminist film criticism. Indeed, recent studies of the zombie film by feminist scholars claim that it "frequently disregard[s] gender for viscera" (MacCormack 104), emphasizing "narrative and visual spaces that create genderless identificatory viewing positions" (Patterson 115). This chapter has shown that far from disregarding issues of sex and gender, zombie movies made in the new millennium have often placed them front and center, addressing them in ways that encourage viewers to identify with women and against the dominant patriarchal order.

If, as Ellen Draper has suggested, the zombie film catered in its earliest incarnations to the male gaze, demonstrating "cinema's capacity for domination, narcissism, and solipsism" (62), it tends today to expose that gaze to critique. Even contemporary softcore and hardcore zombie porn from Rob Rotten's *Porn of the Dead* (2006) to Jay Lee's *Zombie Strippers* (2008) reveals, as Steve Jones writes, the "ideological and discursive pressures that encourage both men and women to behave in ways that subordinate women" ("Porn" 57). This is not to say that twenty-first-century zombie films are uniformly feminist. Clearly that is not the case, even with the movies discussed in this chapter. But in zombifying the romantic comedy and the melodrama, filmmakers have lately turned traditional genres to a recognizably feminist purpose, creating a space for us to contemplate patriarchy as a kind of living death.

CONCLUSION
Homebodies

Looking ahead, the future of zombie cinema increasingly seems to lie in television. This is partly a matter of audience share: zombie TV is quickly eclipsing zombie cinema in popularity. The viewership for a single episode of AMC's *The Walking Dead* (2010–)—a staggering twenty million people watched the season 6 premiere in October 2015, either live or as a recording in the three days that followed (Patten)—dwarfs the audience for all but the biggest zombie blockbusters. And a wave of zombie-themed shows has hit television in recent years, including *Dead Set* (2008), *The Returned* (*Les revenants*, 2012–), *In the Flesh* (2013–2014), *Z Nation* (2014–), *iZombie* (2015–), and *Fear the Walking Dead* (2015–). While none of them has matched the phenomenal level of success enjoyed by *The Walking Dead*, their sheer number suggests a sizeable and growing public appetite for zombie programming. But if television is the future of the zombie film, it's not just because of ratings. In a fundamental sense, zombie

TV represents an evolutionary step forward for zombie cinema. As we've seen in the preceding chapters, zombie movies offer viewers a space to contemplate various aspects of the dominant culture in the West—whiteness, capitalism, patriarchy—as forms of living death. I end this book by proposing that zombie television shows go these films one further, asking us not only to imagine the collapse of that culture but also to consider what might come next.

Zombie TV deconstructs a key trope of zombie cinema: its idea of home. In zombie films dating at least as far back as *Night of the Living Dead* (1968), home is at the center of the story, standing in for the status quo that is under siege and must be defended against the dead. These movies are at their most basic about characters staying put and trying to protect what they have as the zombie apocalypse unfolds. In zombie TV, the apocalypse is over and home has disappeared. Programs like *The Walking Dead* are structured around its absence. They focus on characters who have been dispossessed by the apocalypse, who have lost their homes in one way or another, and as a consequence must constantly stay on the move. By and large, this is not a theme explored in zombie cinema. Kyle William Bishop has observed that a few recent zombie movies, like *Zombieland* (2009) and *World War Z* (2013), feature protagonists who "spend the majority of their narratives on extended 'road trips,' repeatedly locating and abandoning possible safe zones to seek some kind of utopian promised land or site of rescue and redemption" (*How* 23). These films typically end with a homecoming of one sort or another, however. Homecoming is always postponed in zombie TV. No doubt this is in part because of the serialized nature of television, which, as Dan Hassler-Forest notes, tends to privilege an "endlessly deferred narrative" over the "novelistic closure and thematic coherence" associated with cinema (91). But it's also because these shows—designed, ironically, to be watched at home—are in essence about the irrevocable loss of home, the notion that you can't go home again. Briefly surveying three examples of zombie TV in the pages that follow, I argue that this emphasis on dispossession invites us to contemplate the end of the dominant social order in the West, as well as the opportunities for cultural evolution that its disappearance offers.

The theme of dispossession is introduced in spectacular fashion in the first zombie-themed television program of the new millennium, the British miniseries *Dead Set*. Written and produced by Charlie Brooker—the creator of the more recent *Black Mirror* (2011–), a chilling, science-fictional take on technological alienation—and directed by Yann Demange, *Dead Set* originally aired in five episodes on Channel Four in 2008. It envisions a zombie outbreak that interrupts taping of the British reality TV show *Big Brother* (2000–) on an eviction night, when a large crowd of fans has gathered at the studio to see who will be voted out of the house next. The audience and most of the crew are transformed into the living dead, trapping the narcissistic contestants—Marky (Warren Brown), Veronica (Beth Cordingly), Space (Adam Deacon), Angel (Chizzy Akudolu), Grayson (Raj Ghatak), Joplin (Kevin Eldon), and Pippa (Kathleen McDermott)—on the set along with the crass, bullying producer Patrick (Andy Nyman) and his assistant, Kelly (Jaime Winstone). As the housemates fight for their lives, their every move is captured by the still-running cameras and broadcast to a nation that is now populated almost entirely by zombies. Self-reflexive in the extreme—the cast even includes actual stars of *Big Brother*, from then-host Davina McCall to the former contestant Aisleyne Horgan-Wallace to the narrator Marcus Bentley, who essentially play themselves—*Dead Set* can be read, like the media zombie movies discussed in chapter 2, as a commentary on our contemporary society of the spectacle. As Bishop writes, it "cleverly blurs the lines between the real and the fictitious, the simulacra and that being simulated," suggesting a "critique of reality TV, celebrity culture, and mindless audience voyeurism" (*How* 113–114).

But there is more to the show than this. It is a critique not just of television culture but of the dominant culture. Key to that critique is the way in which *Dead Set* deconstructs the notion of home that is central to zombie cinema. Like countless zombie films, the series revolves around the defense of a home against the living dead. Here, though, that home is the patently fake *Big Brother* house, with its tacky studio decor, two-way mirrors, hidden microphones, and ubiquitous cameras. It is a home in name only, lacking any sense of warmth, comfort, or privacy. Indeed, it more closely resembles a prison whose inmates are isolated from the outside world and exposed to constant surveillance, their every move recorded and subject to judgment. This is significant, because insofar as the home stands for society as a whole in zombie cinema, representing everything that survivors fight to protect from the dead, the message we get from *Dead Set* is that society isn't worth saving. The reality TV home it features suggests a society that passes itself off as natural but is completely artificial—an invasive, panoptic culture that polices and disciplines its citizens to ensure they observe the "house rules." Rather than rooting for its defense, the show implies, we should rejoice in its collapse. And this is precisely what Brooker invites us to do. Opening the series with an episode that juxtaposes the latest eviction from the *Big Brother* home with an outbreak of the living dead, he frames the zombie apocalypse as a kind of housecleaning—one in which the contestants' dispossession serves as an allegory for the dismantling of an oppressive social order. Over the course of the four episodes that follow, as the home is gradually reduced to a "dead set" populated only by zombies, it is also emptied of its power and significance as a symbol of the dominant culture.

While the show presents dispossession as a type of liberation, however, it is not something that the characters welcome. Ironically, they remain "dead set" against leaving home despite the oppressiveness of the *Big Brother* house and the social order it represents. If it's effectively a prison, they prove to be willing inmates. This is perhaps not surprising where the contestants are concerned. After all, they signed up for life in the house, happily exchanging their freedom and privacy for a shot at fame. Their commitment to the dominant culture is also evident in the way they have re-created its racial, sexual, and gender hierarchies in the home, with a popular white couple—fit, young "chavs" Marky and Veronica—lording it over everyone else, especially the transgender Indian Grayson and the African immigrant Angel. It is little wonder, then, that when the zombie apocalypse hits, they stay put, treating it as an extension of the *Big Brother* game—sizing up rivals, forming alliances, voting on key decisions, completing challenges, and vying to be the lone survivor, all while obsessing over how they look on television.

More surprising is the fact that the show's "outsiders" are just as anxious to hold onto the house, particularly the tough, resourceful production assistant Kelly, who is the focal point of the series and who should have a more skeptical view of life in the home given her work behind the scenes on *Big Brother*. But when she gains access to the set after the outbreak, she quickly embraces life as the newest "housemate," bonding in particular with the disaffected Arab contestant Space. The same is true of her boyfriend, Riq (Riz Ahmed), when he makes his way to the studio after seeing Kelly on TV. Oddly enough, the piggish producer Patrick is the only one with enough sense to leave—and he is prevented from doing so by the others, who debate whether they should kill him or simply break his ankles to make him stay. Of course, Patrick's instincts prove correct in the end; the zombies finally break into the home and "turn" all of its inhabitants. The final shots of the series capture the undead contestants milling listlessly about the demolished set. As literal "homebodies," they underscore the satirical point of the show: in the wake of the zombie apocalypse, there literally is no place like home. We cling to the old social order at our own peril.

No doubt in part because of *Dead Set*'s limited run as a miniseries, it doesn't really envisage what lies beyond the home; however, subsequent examples of zombie television have. If Brooker's show focuses on clearing away the last vestiges of the dominant culture, they focus on what might follow it. Tellingly, rather than imagining an alternative social order, many picture postapocalyptic existence as a kind of perpetual flux in which society and individuals alike are always engaged in the process of becoming, never stuck in a state of being. They depict dispossession as rich with possibility, privileging change over stasis.

That is certainly the case with *The Returned*, a French TV series created in 2012 by Fabrice Gobert. Inspired by Robin Campillo's film *They Came Back* (*Les revenants*, 2004), this haunting and elliptical show tells the story of a small town in the mountains whose dead one day mysteriously began to return from the grave. Looking and behaving much the same as they did before, but with no memory of their deaths, they seek to rejoin their families and resume their old lives. The first season, jointly directed by Gobert and Frédéric Mermoud, initially seems to memorialize the idea of homecoming. Each of the early episodes is devoted to the arrival home of one of the "returned." Four years after tragically dying in a school-bus crash, the teenage Camille (Yara Pilartz) is reunited with her parents, Claire (Anne Consigny) and Jérôme (Frédéric Pierrot), and her twin sister, Lena (Jenna Thiam). The moody rock musician Simon (Pierre Perrier), who committed suicide on the eve of his wedding a decade earlier, returns to his former fiancée, Adèle (Clotilde Hesme). Thirty years after accidentally drowning in the town's lake, the middle-aged Madame Costa (Laetitia de Fombelle) is brought back to her now-elderly husband. And, more disturbingly, the serial killer Serge (Guillaume Gouix) comes home to his brother Toni (Grégory Gadebois), who clubbed him to death seven years before in order to stop his murder of young women.

But it quickly becomes clear that a true homecoming isn't possible for these zombies. Their homes still stand, their loved ones are still there, but the dead no longer fit into their old lives. Camille discovers to her horror that her parents, driven apart by their grief over her death, are now divorced; moreover, her twin sister, now four years older than she, is like a different person. Simon finds that Adèle has moved on: she is now the mother of a ten-year-old daughter, Chloé (Brune Martin), and engaged to a local police officer, Thomas (Samir Guesmi). When Madame Costa returns, her terrified husband ties her up, torches their home with her in it, and then kills himself. And upon seeing Serge again, Toni promptly brains him with a shovel and locks him out of the house.

Although the dead have been restored to life, they cannot truly come home. Nor can they leave town, as a mysterious force keeps them in the area. Physically and ontologically, they are in a kind of limbo. Some are adopted by kind strangers: Victor (Swann Nambotin), a boy who was killed decades earlier in a home invasion and may be responsible for the return of the dead, is taken in by a lonely nurse, Julie (Céline Sallette). Others wind up at a local shelter run by Pierre (Jean-François Sivadier), who believes that the zombies' arrival is a sign of end times. Ultimately, however, their profound homelessness heralds the emergence of a new mode of existence. The first season of the series ends with the appearance of a larger group of zombies that has been subsisting in the woods surrounding the town. Led by a messianic medium named Lucy (Ana Girardot), the "horde," as it is called in the show, absorbs the rest of the dead and returns to the forest to pursue a wholly nomadic life. Meanwhile, the nearby lake floods, inundating the town and forcing many of its inhabitants from their homes—an apocalyptic sign that dispossession will not be limited to the returned.

Indeed, in the delayed second season of *The Returned*, which aired in 2015 and was codirected by Gobert and Frédéric Goupil, the loss of home becomes universal, precipitating the complete breakdown of social order. Picking up some six months after the events that ended the first season, the show reveals that the flood has profoundly altered life in the town. Much of it remains submerged, and many of its residents have left, giving it the look of a ghost town. Those who have stayed are forced to dwell in temporary housing or in their own waterlogged houses, which, shrouded in plastic sheeting and filled with debris, no longer feel like home. Although the residents lead a makeshift, provisional existence similar to that adopted by the zombies, they have not embraced it. In fact, many have joined a quasi-fascist cult led by Pierre, the manager of the local shelter, who holds the dead responsible for the town's woes and is determined to hunt them down. He and his reactionary followers are fanatically dedicated to what, borrowing from Gilles Deleuze and Félix Guattari, might be called "reterritorialization": the restoration not just of the town's homes but of its normative social order.

The dead, for their part, remain resolutely committed to deterritorialization. They have taken over an empty neighborhood that was cut off from the rest of the town by the flood and is accessible only by boat. Occupying abandoned houses with no running water or electricity, they give the impression not of being "at home" but of temporarily squatting. And they are joined by more zombies every day, including two more teens who died in the same school-bus crash as Camille, Victor's mother and brother, and Serge and Toni's father. The season seems to build toward a climactic confrontation between the horde and Pierre's faction of fanatics. But the expected clash doesn't come. Instead, Pierre's brutal tactics (which include the imprisonment and torture of the zombies he manages to capture) eventually alienate his followers, who desert him, while the dead are again unified and galvanized into movement by Lucy, with the help of a unique baby born to Simon and Adèle. The season's typically enigmatic but resonant finale, which concludes with the horde commencing the next phase of its migration, confirms that the show's sympathies are firmly on the side of deterritorialization—quite literally, there is no contest. It stands as a celebration of perpetual dispossession and the virtues of contingency and change.

The same is true of the most popular zombie show currently on TV: *The Walking Dead*. Based on a graphic-novel series created by Robert Kirkman and developed for the cable channel AMC by the filmmaker Frank Darabont (who was replaced as showrunner after the first season, initially by Glen Mazzara and then by Scott M. Gimple), it, too, takes permanent dispossession as its central theme. The show, which over its six seasons to date has followed the efforts of the small-town Georgia sheriff's deputy Rick Grimes (Andrew Lincoln) to keep his family and a ragtag band of survivors alive in the wake of a zombie apocalypse, is often described as a modern-day western. It's easy to see why. The postapocalyptic South depicted in the series resembles the Old West in its untamed wildness. And Rick, at least early on, calls to mind the western hero, with his unswerving moral rectitude, sheriff's deputy uniform and campaign hat, and six-gun holstered on his hip. He even mounts a horse to ride into a deserted Atlanta in an iconic moment at the end of the series premiere.

But on a deeper, thematic level, the kinship between *The Walking Dead* and the western breaks down. If, as Thomas Schatz argues, the western in its classic form revolves around a contest between civilization and savagery in which "the values, attitudes, and ideals associated with westward expansion and the taming and civilizing of the West" finally prevail (46), then *The Walking Dead* might be more accurately described as an antiwestern. The show chronicles the triumph of disorder over order, savagery over civilization. It does so partly through its deconstruction of the traditional western hero, who is defined by his "moral commitment to civilization" and works to "ensure social order" (Schatz 51, 63). Shelley S. Rees observes that by the middle of the second season, the series has framed Rick's "stubborn commitment to the ideology of the old world" as a dangerous delusion, thus "disempowering its Western-infused protagonist and the values associated with him" (83, 87). And when Rick abandons that ideology in later seasons, electing to defend his band of survivors by any means necessary, the show strips him of all authority as an agent of civilization, reducing him to "a man wielding influence through guns and acts of violence" (Young 65).

In my view, however, *The Walking Dead*'s deconstruction of the traditional western hero is not the only—or even the main—way in which it overturns the western's privileging of civilization over savagery. It also does so through its emphasis on the dispossession of its characters. The loss of home looms large in the series, serving as a central metaphor for the disappearance of the old social order and the formlessness of life after the zombie apocalypse. The first season begins with Rick abandoning his own home when he wakes from a coma to find his town devastated by a zombie outbreak and his wife, Lori (Sarah Wayne Callies), and young son, Carl (Chandler Riggs), missing; it ends with him reunited with his family and the leader of a group of survivors but deprived of the very notion of home. Having traveled to the Centers for Disease Control and Prevention in Atlanta, he and his followers learn not only that there is no known cure for the zombie virus but also that they are all already infected— meaning that when they die, they will "turn" regardless of whether they've been bitten or not. Civilization is over;

postapocalyptic existence will unfold in the wilderness, defined by life on the open road.

As if to underscore this point, each subsequent season of the show has been structured around the group's discovery and loss of a potential home. In season 2, they find refuge at a farm tended by Hershel Greene (Scott Wilson) and his family but are forced into flight again when it is overrun by the dead. In season 3, they take shelter in a deserted prison but are driven out by a rival group under the sway of the sociopathic Governor (David Morissey). In season 4, they follow signs promising sanctuary to a town called Terminus but discover when they arrive that it is run by cannibals who slaughter and cook their guests. In season 5, they head to Washington, D.C., after meeting a scientist named Eugene (Josh McDermitt) who claims to have found a cure for the zombie virus but stop short when he admits he lied to ensure his protection. And in season 6, the most recent at the time of this writing, they are welcomed into the seemingly idyllic Alexandria Safe Zone, only to see it compromised by two outside factions, the feral Wolves and the extortionist Saviors. Again and again, the show withholds the western's promise of civilization from its characters, ensuring that their lives differ little from those of its wandering dead, who, significantly, are known not as "zombies" but as "walkers."

While this rootlessness is tragic from a certain (largely nostalgic and reactionary) point of view, the series also presents it as fraught with possibility. Unfettered by the old social order, the show's characters are free to develop in ways they never would have under the dominant culture in place before the zombie apocalypse. It's true that not all of them change for the better. Rick has devolved from a just and compassionate man into a despot and a killer who by the sixth season doesn't hesitate to order a bloody, preemptive strike against another group of survivors that *may* represent a threat. But his transformation has not been linear or complete. It has been characterized by stops, starts, hesitations, and reversals that suggest the potential for future change in any direction. Moreover, his devolution has been balanced by the evolution of other key characters. For example, the stoic, crossbow-toting Daryl (Norman Reedus), perhaps the show's most popular character, has developed from a bigoted redneck into a selfless hero. Likewise, Carol (Melissa McBride), who went from an abused wife to a ruthless enforcer early in the series, has recently renounced violence entirely.

It's important to note, as well, that the show highlights how the zombie apocalypse has enabled the rise of individuals marginalized by the old social order. It has been criticized for the frequency with which it kills off non-white characters—particularly black men like T-Dog

(IronE Singleton) and Tyreese (Chad Coleman)—but it should also be recognized for the central roles it gives those like the formidable, katana-wielding Michonne (Danai Gurira) and the scrappy, resourceful Glenn (Steven Yeun), whose interracial romance with Maggie (Lauren Cohan) has become the heart of the series. In *The Walking Dead*, dispossession and the fall of civilization, for all their hardships, serve to amplify female, black, Asian, Latino, gay, and lesbian voices, demonstrating once again that the perpetual flux of postapocalyptic existence has a progressive dimension. Like other examples of zombie TV, the show—a product of the comic creator Kirkman's desire to devise "a zombie movie that never ends" (iv)—opens a space through its serialization for us to contemplate not only what we are but also who we might become. Looking beyond the zombie apocalypse, it imagines a future for zombie cinema.

Of course, the future of zombie cinema—and zombie culture more broadly—isn't guaranteed. Some scholars already see signs that the twenty-first-century zombie renaissance is winding down. Sarah Juliet Lauro declares in her recent, superb book *The Transatlantic Zombie* that "the era of the millennial zombie is over" (2). But as I write this in mid-2016, zombie culture seems as vital and robust as ever. The living dead still haunt the popular imagination. In just the past few weeks, a video of a trio of brothers tricking their little sister—who is spacey from pain medication after the removal of her wisdom teeth—into believing there has been a zombie outbreak in Washington, D.C., has racked up over twenty million views on YouTube; a story about a Nashville man battling his homeowners association to keep a zombie statue in his front yard has received national coverage; and news that a Philadelphia-based company called Bioquark is looking for ways to "reanimate" the brain-dead has sparked widespread fears of an imminent zombie apocalypse. Zombie fandom continues to thrive as well. Websites like the Zombie Research Society and social media outlets like the Zombies Facebook page still flourish, dispensing information about the living dead and tips for surviving the zombie apocalypse to a global audience. The Walker Stalker Con and other zombie conventions still draw large crowds in cities like Chicago, Boston, Philadelphia, Atlanta, and London. And thousands of people still gather in drag as the dead to stage Zombie Walks around the world, from San Antonio and Louisville to Sitges and Tel Aviv.

The zombie economy, too, continues to boom. The dead remain hugely popular in video games across a variety of platforms and genres, with new installments forthcoming in such hit franchises as *Dead Island*, *Left 4 Dead*, and *Resident Evil*. Players also eagerly await the next stage in the zombie video game's evolution: virtual reality. Several virtual-reality zombie games are currently in the works, including *Arizona Sunshine* and *The Brookhaven Experiment*, which are being developed for the HTC Vive by Vertigo Games and Phosphor Games, respectively. The dead remain popular in fiction as well, with new books regularly appearing from established zombie authors like Brian Keene, Mira Grant, Carrie Ryan, and Jonathan Maberry, the latter of whom has announced that he and George A. Romero will coedit a zombie anthology titled *Horror of the Living Dead* featuring stories set after the events depicted in Romero's *Night of the Living Dead*. Meanwhile, zombie comics and graphic novels still sell briskly, with Kirkman's *The Walking Dead*—now past its 150th issue—joined by other established series like Mark Kidwell's *'68* and Tim Seeley's *Revival* and new efforts like Stephen Romano and Shawn Lewis's illustrated version of Lucio Fulci's *Zombie* (*Zombi 2*, 1979). As I noted at the outset of this conclusion, zombie TV has exploded in recent years. *The Walking Dead*, in particular, has become something of a cultural institution, spawning toys, merchandise, cruises, and a new attraction at the Universal Studios Hollywood theme park; it is far from the only hit zombie show, however, as ratings for *iZombie* and *Fear the Walking Dead* demonstrate. And driving it all is zombie cinema, which has continued to thrive as the genre has gone global and Hollywood has doubled down on the dead, announcing sequels to *Zombieland* and *World War Z*, as well as adaptations of Stephen King's *Cell: A Novel* and Carrie Ryan's *The Forest of Hands and Teeth*, among other upcoming productions.

The twenty-first-century zombie renaissance will undoubtedly end at some point. And in the cyclical fashion of all genres, zombie cinema will eventually fall out of favor with audiences. Until then, though, it presents those of us living in the West, especially, with a unique opportunity to examine ourselves and our culture. Scholars have generally suggested that the contemporary zombie apocalypse is rooted in our fears of (or desires for) the Other. I have argued throughout this book, to the contrary, that the dead are popular today because we (finally) recognize ourselves in them. If monsters are, to quote Judith Halberstam, "meaning machines" (21), the meaning of the zombie in the new millennium is that we are the monsters. On one level, this is perhaps obvious. As Kim Paffenroth puts it, "With a monster that is so fully and banally human, one interpretation that will surely always be open and likely, is that the zombies are us—not the mysterious or reviled 'other,' however that is constructed—but us, in all our hungry, grasping, mindless simplicity. We will always be our worst enemies, and the ones we can never fully eliminate" (24). But I have endeavored to show that we share a deeper kinship with the dead, one that has allowed them to function in cinema as a sort of funhouse mirror for dominant Western culture, reflecting the deathliness of whiteness, capitalism, and patriarchy. One could conclude on the basis of the zombie film's current popularity that we have simply accepted our deathliness as a society—that we respond to the "chaotic exhilaration of collapse" offered by zombie cinema because it "speaks to what we might call a *social* death drive" (Sconce 106). I prefer to think that we have embraced the dead because zombie cinema, at its best, not only forces us to confront our own deathliness but also enables us to imagine ourselves free of it. Razing the old social order, it invites us to envision something better in its place. This, in my view, is ultimately what explains our seemingly insatiable appetite for the dead today. They don't just reflect who we are; they illuminate what we can become.

ACKNOWLEDGMENTS

No book is completed without the encouragement and support of others—even a relatively brief volume like this one. There are a number of people I need to thank for assisting me as I wrote *Zombie Cinema*. First, my thanks to series editors Gwendolyn Audrey Foster and Wheeler Winston Dixon, who along with editor in chief Leslie Mitchner provided invaluable guidance as I shaped the book in manuscript. Its inclusion in the Quick Takes series at Rutgers University Press is an honor. I'm grateful to my department chair, Victor Taylor, and academic dean, Dominic DelliCarpini, at York College of Pennsylvania for granting me a course release to work on this project. I'm also grateful to the students in the class on zombie cinema I taught at York in the spring of 2016 as I wrote the book; their enthusiasm for the subject and sharp insights into the movies we watched were sources of inspiration. Finally, and most importantly, I owe a debt of gratitude that can never be paid to God, who showed me the way forward, and to my family—Jill, Ethan, and Emma—who gave me the strength I needed to take it.

FURTHER READING

Balaji, Murali, ed. *Thinking Dead: What the Zombie Apoca-*
lypse Means. Lanham, MD: Lexington, 2013.

Bishop, Kyle William. *American Zombie Gothic: The Rise and*
Fall (and Rise) of the Walking Dead in Popular Culture.
Jefferson, NC: McFarland, 2010.

——. *How Zombies Conquered Popular Culture: The Multi-*
farious Walking Dead in the 21st Century. Jefferson, NC:
McFarland, 2015.

Boluk, Stephanie, and Wylie Lenz, eds. *Generation Zombie:*
Essays on the Living Dead in Modern Culture. Jefferson,
NC: McFarland, 2011.

Brottman, Mikita. *Meat Is Murder! An Illustrated Guide to*
Cannibal Culture. New ed. London: Creation, 2001.

Castillo, David R., David Schmid, David A. Reilly, and John
Edgar Browning. *Zombie Talk: Culture, History, Politics.*
Basingstoke, UK: Palgrave Macmillan, 2016.

Christie, Deborah, and Sarah Juliet Lauro, eds. *Better Off*
Dead: The Evolution of the Zombie as Posthuman. New
York: Fordham UP, 2011.

Comentale, Edward P., and Aaron Jaffe, eds. *The Year's Work*
at the Zombie Research Center. Bloomington: Indiana UP,
2014.

Grant, Barry Keith, and Christopher Sharrett, eds. *Planks of*

Reason: Essays on the Horror Film. Rev. ed. Lanham, MD: Scarecrow, 2004.

Hubner, Laura, Marcus Leaning, and Paul Manning, eds. *The Zombie Renaissance in Popular Culture.* Basingstoke, UK: Palgrave Macmillan, 2015.

Hunt, Leon, Sharon Lockyer, and Milly Williamson, eds. *Screening the Undead: Vampires and Zombies in Film and Television.* London: I. B. Tauris, 2014.

Lauro, Sarah Juliet. *The Transatlantic Zombie: Slavery, Rebellion, and Living Death.* New Brunswick, NJ: Rutgers UP, 2015.

Luckhurst, Roger. *Zombies: A Cultural History.* London: Reaktion, 2015.

McGlotten, Shaka, and Steve Jones, eds. *Zombies and Sexuality: Essays on Desire and the Living Dead.* Jefferson, NC: McFarland, 2014.

McIntosh, Shawn, and Marc Leverette, eds. *Zombie Culture: Autopsies of the Living Dead.* Lanham, MD: Scarecrow, 2008.

Moreman, Christopher M., and Cory James Rushton, eds. *Race, Oppression, and the Zombie: Essays on Cross-Cultural Appropriations of the Caribbean Tradition.* Jefferson, NC: McFarland, 2011.

———, eds. *Zombies Are Us: Essays on the Humanity of the Walking Dead.* Jefferson, NC: McFarland, 2011.

Russell, Jamie. *Book of the Dead: The Complete History of Zombie Cinema.* Rev. ed. London: Titan, 2014.

WORKS CITED

Ackermann, Hans-W., and Jeanine Gauthier. "The Ways and Nature of the Zombi." *Journal of American Folklore* 104.414 (1991): 466–494. Print.

Altman, Rick. *Film/Genre*. London: BFI, 1999. Print.

Bansak, Edmund G. *Fearing the Dark: The Val Lewton Career*. Jefferson, NC: McFarland, 1995. Print.

Bartolovich, Crystal. "Consumerism, or the Cultural Logic of Late Cannibalism." *Cannibalism and the Colonial World*. Ed. Francis Barker, Peter Hulme, and Margaret Iversen. Cambridge: Cambridge UP, 1998. 204–237. Print.

Baudrillard, Jean. *Simulacra and Simulation*. Trans. Sheila Faria Glaser. Ann Arbor: U of Michigan P, 1994. Print.

Benshoff, Harry M. "Blaxploitation Horror Films: Generic Reappropriation or Reinscription?" *Cinema Journal* 39.2 (2000): 31–50. Print.

Bishop, Kyle William. "Dead Man Still Walking: Explaining the Zombie Renaissance." *Journal of Popular Film and Television* 37.1 (2009): 17–25. Print.

———. *How Zombies Conquered Popular Culture: The Multifarious Walking Dead in the 21st Century*. Jefferson, NC: McFarland, 2015. Print.

Bishop, Kyle William. "Raising the Dead: Unearthing the Nonliterary Origins of Zombie Cinema." *Journal of Popular Film and Television* 33.4 (2006): 196–205. Print.

———. "The Sub-Subaltern Monster: Imperialist Hegemony and the Cinematic Voodoo Zombie." *Journal of American Culture* 31.2 (2008): 141–152. Print.

Black Jesus. "We're All Zombies Now." *Everything Black, Everything Dead.* Grindhead Records, 2014. MP3.

Bosch, Torie. "First, Eat All the Lawyers." *Slate* 25 Oct. 2011. Web. 14 Nov. 2015.

Charity, Tom. "All the Rage." *Danny Boyle: Interviews.* Ed. Brent Dunham. Jackson: UP of Mississippi, 2011. 70–73. Print.

Clover, Carol J. *Men, Women, and Chain Saws: Gender in the Modern Horror Film.* Princeton, NJ: Princeton UP, 1992. Print.

Coleman, Robin R. Means. *Horror Noire: Blacks in American Horror Films from the 1890s to Present.* New York: Routledge, 2011. Print.

Davis, Wade. *Passage of Darkness: The Ethnobiology of the Haitian Zombie.* Chapel Hill: U of North Carolina P, 1988. Print.

Dayan, Joan. *Haiti, History, and the Gods.* Berkeley: U of California P, 1995. Print.

Debord, Guy. *The Society of the Spectacle.* Trans. Donald Nicholson-Smith. New York: Zone, 1995. Print.

Deleuze, Gilles, and Félix Guattari. *Anti-Oedipus: Capitalism and Schizophrenia.* Trans. Robert Hurley, Mark Seem, and Helen R. Lane. Minneapolis: U of Minnesota P, 1983. Print.

Dendle, Peter. "The Zombie as Barometer of Cultural Anxiety." *Monsters and the Monstrous: Myths and Metaphors of Enduring Evil*. Ed. Niall Scott. Amsterdam: Rodopi, 2007. 45–57. Print.

Dixon, Wheeler Winston. *Streaming: Movies, Media, and Instant Access*. Lexington: UP of Kentucky, 2013. Print.

Doane, Mary Ann. *The Desire to Desire: The Woman's Film of the 1940s*. Bloomington: Indiana UP, 1987. Print.

Doherty, Thomas. *Pre-Code Hollywood: Sex, Immorality, and Insurrection in American Cinema, 1930–1934*. New York: Columbia UP, 1999. Print.

Drake, Michael S. "Zombinations: Reading the Undead as Debt and Guilt in the National Imaginary." *Monster Culture in the 21st Century: A Reader*. Ed. Marina Levina and Diem-My T. Bui. London: Bloomsbury, 2013. 229–241. Print.

Draper, Ellen. "Zombie Women When the Gaze Is Male." *Wide Angle* 10.3 (1988): 52–62. Print.

Dyer, Richard. *White*. London: Routledge, 1997. Print.

Dyson, Emma. "Diaries of a Plague Year: Perspectives of Destruction in Contemporary Zombie Film." *Screening the Undead: Vampires and Zombies in Film and Television*. Ed. Leon Hunt, Sharon Lockyer, and Milly Williamson. London: I. B. Tauris, 2014. 131–147. Print.

Fanon, Frantz. *Black Skin, White Masks*. Trans. Charles Lam Markmann. New York: Grove, 1967. Print.

Foster, Gwendolyn Audrey. "The Corruption of the Family and the Disease of Whiteness in *I Walked with a Zombie*." *A Family Affair: Cinema Calls Home*. Ed. Murray Pomerance. London: Wallflower, 2008. 149–160. Print.

Foster, Gwendolyn Audrey. *Hoarders, Doomsday Preppers, and the Culture of Apocalypse*. New York: Palgrave Macmillan, 2014. Print.

Fujiwara, Chris. *Jacques Tourneur: The Cinema of Nightfall*. Baltimore: Johns Hopkins UP, 1998. Print.

Halberstam, Judith. *Skin Shows: Gothic Horror and the Technology of Monsters*. Durham, NC: Duke UP, 1995. Print.

Hassler-Forest, Dan. "*The Walking Dead*: Quality Television, Transmedia Serialization, and Zombies." *Serialization in Popular Culture*. Ed. Rob Allen and Thijs van den Berg. New York: Routledge, 2014. 91–105. Print.

Heller-Nicholas, Alexandra. *Rape-Revenge Films: A Critical Study*. Jefferson, NC: McFarland, 2011. Print.

Hunter, Russ. "Nightmare Cities: Italian Zombie Cinema and Environmental Discourses." *Screening the Undead: Vampires and Zombies in Film and Television*. Ed. Leon Hunt, Sharon Lockyer, and Milly Williamson. London: I. B. Tauris, 2014. 112–130. Print.

Jacobs, Lea. *The Wages of Sin: Censorship and the Fallen Woman Film, 1928–1942*. Madison: U of Wisconsin P, 1991. Print.

Jones, Steve. "Gender Monstrosity: *Deadgirl* and the Sexual Politics of Zombie-Rape." *Feminist Media Studies* 13.3 (2013): 525–539. Print.

———. "Porn of the Dead: Necrophilia, Feminism, and Gendering the Undead." *Zombies Are Us: Essays on the Humanity of the Walking Dead*. Ed. Christopher M. Moreman and Cory James Rushton. Jefferson, NC: McFarland, 2011. 40–61. Print.

Kee, Chera. "'They Are Not Men . . . They Are Dead Bod-
ies!': From Cannibal to Zombie and Back Again." *Better
Off Dead: The Evolution of the Zombie as Post-Human.*
Ed. Deborah Christie and Sarah Juliet Lauro. New York:
Fordham UP, 2011. 9–23. Print.

Keough, Peter. "Interview with George Romero." *George A.
Romero: Interviews.* Ed. Tony Williams. Jackson: UP of
Mississippi, 2011. 169–177. Print.

Kilgour, Maggie. "The Function of Cannibalism at the
Present Time." *Cannibalism and the Colonial World.* Ed.
Francis Barker, Peter Hulme, and Margaret Iversen.
Cambridge: Cambridge UP, 1998. 238–259. Print.

Kirkman, Robert. Introduction. *The Walking Dead, Volume
1: Days Gone Bye.* By Robert Kirkman and Tony Moore.
Berkeley, CA: Image Comics, 2007. i–iv. Print.

Kissell, Rick. "'Fear the Walking Dead' Sets All-Time Cable
Ratings Premiere Record." *Variety* 24 Aug. 2015. Web. 13
Nov. 2015.

Klein, Ezra. "The Most Predictable Disaster in the History
of the Human Race." *Vox* 27 May 2015. Web. 29 Nov. 2015.

Krutnik, Frank. "Conforming Passions? Contemporary
Romantic Comedy." *Genre and Contemporary Hollywood.*
Ed. Steve Neale. London: BFI, 2002. 130–147. Print.

Laist, Randy. "Soft Murders: Motion Pictures and Living
Death in *Diary of the Dead.*" *Generation Zombie: Essays on
the Living Dead in Modern Culture.* Ed. Stephanie Boluk
and Wylie Lenz. Jefferson, NC: McFarland, 2011. 101–112.
Print.

LaPlace, Maria. "Producing and Consuming the Woman's
Film: Discursive Struggle in *Now, Voyager.*" *Home Is*

Where the Heart Is: Studies in Melodrama and the Woman's Film. Ed. Christine Gledhill. London: BFI, 1987. 138–166. Print.

Lauro, Sarah Juliet. "The Eco-Zombie: Environmental Critique in Zombie Fiction." *Generation Zombie: Essays on the Living Dead in Modern Culture*. Ed. Stephanie Boluk and Wylie Lenz. Jefferson, NC: McFarland, 2011. 54–66. Print.

———. *The Transatlantic Zombie: Slavery, Rebellion, and Living Death*. New Brunswick, NJ: Rutgers UP, 2015. Print.

Lehman, Peter. "'Don't Blame This on a Girl': Female Rape-Revenge Films." *Screening the Male: Exploring Masculinities in Hollywood Cinema*. Ed. Steven Cohan and Ina Rae Hark. London: Routledge, 1993. 103–117. Print.

Lenz, Christian. "Love Your Zombie: Romancing the Undead." *Collision of Realities: Establishing Research on the Fantastic in Europe*. Ed. Lars Schmeink and Astrid Böger. Berlin: De Gruyter, 2012. 103–117. Print.

Lutz, John. "Zombies of the World, Unite: Class Struggle and Alienation in *Land of the Dead*." *The Philosophy of Horror*. Ed. Thomas Fahy. Lexington: UP of Kentucky, 2010. 121–136. Print.

MacCormack, Patricia. *Cinesexuality*. Aldershot, UK: Ashgate, 2008. Print.

Marx, Karl. *Capital*. Vol. 1. Trans. Ben Fowkes. Harmondsworth, UK: Penguin, 1976. Print.

McAlister, Elizabeth A. *Rara! Vodou, Power, and Performance in Haiti and Its Diaspora*. Berkeley: U of California P, 2002. Print.

McDonald, Tamar Jeffers. *Romantic Comedy: Boy Meets Girl Meets Genre*. London: Wallflower, 2007. Print.

Morrison, Alan. "Rage against the Machine." *Empire* 161 (2002): 98–105. Print.

Muntean, Nick, and Matthew Thomas Payne. "Attack of the Livid Dead: Recalibrating Terror in the Post–September 11 Zombie Film." *The War on Terror and American Popular Culture: September 11 and Beyond*. Ed. Andrew Schopp and Matthew B. Hill. Madison, NJ: Fairleigh Dickinson UP, 2009. 239–258. Print.

Neale, Steve. "The Big Romance or Something Wild? Romantic Comedy Today." *Screen* 33.3 (1992): 284–299. Print.

Negra, Diane. *What a Girl Wants? Fantasizing the Reclamation of Self in Postfeminism*. Abingdon, UK: Routledge, 2009. Print.

Newitz, Annalee. *Pretend We're Dead: Capitalist Monsters in American Pop Culture*. Durham, NC: Duke UP, 2006. Print.

Newman, Kim. *Nightmare Movies: A Critical Guide to Contemporary Horror Films*. New York: Harmony, 1988. Print.

Nietzsche, Friedrich. *Beyond Good and Evil*. Trans. R. J. Hollingdale. London: Penguin, 1990. Print.

Ogg, John C. "Zombies Worth Over $5 Billion to Economy." *24/7 Wall St.* 25 Oct. 2011. Web. 14 Nov. 2015.

Olney, Ian. *Euro Horror: Classic European Horror Cinema in Contemporary American Culture*. Bloomington: Indiana UP, 2013. Print.

The Originals. "Supernatural Voodoo Woman (Pt. 1)." *Game Called Love*. Soul, 1974. MP3.

Paffenroth, Kim. "Zombies as Internal Fear or Threat." *Generation Zombie: Essays on the Living Dead in Modern Culture*. Ed. Stephanie Boluk and Wylie Lenz. Jefferson, NC: McFarland, 2011. 18–26. Print.

Patten, Dominic. "'Walking Dead' Ratings Hit Almost 20M Viewers for Season 6 Debut in Live + 3." *Deadline Hollywood* 16 Oct. 2015. Web. 15 May 2016.

Patterson, Natasha. "Cannibalizing Gender and Genre: A Feminist Re-vision of George Romero's Zombie Films." *Zombie Culture: Autopsies of the Living Dead*. Ed. Shawn McIntosh and Marc Leverette. Lanham, MD: Scarecrow, 2008. 103–118. Print.

Phillips, Gyllian. "*White Zombie* and the Creole: William Seabrook's *The Magic Island* and American Imperialism in Haiti." *Generation Zombie: Essays on the Living Dead in Modern Culture*. Ed. Stephanie Boluk and Wylie Lenz. Jefferson, NC: McFarland, 2011. 27–40. Print.

Rees, Shelley S. "Frontier Values Meet Big-City Zombies: The Old West in AMC's *The Walking Dead*." *Undead in the West: Vampires, Zombies, Mummies, and Ghosts on the Cinematic Frontier*. Ed. Cynthia J. Miller and A. Bowdoin Van Riper. Lanham, MD: Scarecrow, 2012. 80–94. Print.

Rhodes, Gary D. *White Zombie: Anatomy of a Horror Film*. Jefferson, NC: McFarland, 2001. Print.

Russell, Jamie. *Book of the Dead: The Complete History of Zombie Cinema*. Rev. ed. London: Titan, 2014. Print.

Ruthven, Andrea. "Zombie Postfeminism." *The Year's Work at the Zombie Research Center*. Ed. Edward P. Comentale and Aaron Jaffe. Bloomington: Indiana UP, 2014. 341–360. Print.

Saunders, Robert A. "Undead Spaces: Fear, Globalisation, and the Popular Geopolitics of Zombiism." *Geopolitics* 17.1 (2012): 80–104. Print.

Schatz, Thomas. *Hollywood Genres: Formulas, Filmmaking, and the Studio System.* New York: Random House, 1981. Print.

Sconce, Jeffrey. "Dead Metaphors / Undead Allegories." *Screening the Undead: Vampires and Zombies in Film and Television.* Ed. Leon Hunt, Sharon Lockyer, and Milly Williamson. London: I. B. Tauris, 2014. 95–111. Print.

Seabrook, William. *The Magic Island.* New York: Harcourt, Brace, 1929. Print.

Shapiro, Stephen. "Zombie Health Care." *The Year's Work at the Zombie Research Center.* Ed. Edward P. Comentale and Aaron Jaffe. Bloomington: Indiana UP, 2014. 193–226. Print.

Sharrett, Christopher. "The Idea of Apocalypse in *The Texas Chainsaw Massacre*." *Planks of Reason: Essays on the Horror Film.* Rev. ed. Ed. Barry Keith Grant and Christopher Sharrett. Lanham, MD: Scarecrow, 2004. 300–320. Print.

Shaviro, Steven. *The Cinematic Body.* Minneapolis: U of Minnesota P, 1993. Print.

Skal, David J. *The Monster Show: A Cultural History of Horror.* New York: Penguin, 1993. Print.

St. John, Allen. "'The Walking Dead' Season 5 Premiere Breaks Ratings Record as the Most Watched Cable Show of All Time." *Forbes* 13 Oct. 2014. Web. 13 Nov. 2015.

Walsh, Andrea S. *Women's Film and Female Experience, 1940–1950.* New York: Praeger, 1984. Print.

Williams, Linda. "Film Bodies: Gender, Genre, and Excess." *Film Quarterly* 44.4 (1991): 2–13. Print.

Williams, Tony. *Hearths of Darkness: The Family in the American Horror Film*. Madison, NJ: Fairleigh Dickinson UP, 1996. Print.

Wood, Robin. *Hollywood from Vietnam to Reagan . . . and Beyond*. New York: Columbia UP, 2003. Print.

———. "An Introduction to the American Horror Film." *American Nightmare: Essays on the Horror Film*. Ed. Robin Wood and Richard Lippe. Toronto: Festival of Festivals, 1979. 7–28. Print.

Yakir, Dan. "Mourning Becomes Romero." *Film Comment* 15.3 (1979): 60–65. Print.

Young, P. Ivan. "Walking Tall or Walking Dead? The American Cowboy in the Zombie Apocalypse." *"We're All Infected": Essays on AMC's "The Walking Dead" and the Fate of the Human*. Ed. Dawn Keetley. Jefferson, NC: McFarland, 2014. 56–67. Print.

INDEX

ABOUT THE AUTHOR

Ian Olney is an associate professor of English at York College of Pennsylvania. He is also the author of *Euro Horror: Classic European Horror Cinema in Contemporary American Culture*.

DATE DUE			